MW01644001

Collecting Life

Collecting Life:
Poets on Objects Known and Imagined

Edited by

Madelyn Garner

and

Andrea L. Watson

3: A Taos Press

www.3taospress.com

Published by 3: A Taos Press

ISBN: 9780984792504

First U.S. edition 2011

Book Design: Michele Braverman, BraveStudio, Denver, CO
Press Logo Design: William Watson, Castro Watson, New York, NY
Cover Artwork: Published by permission of the Estate of Bradley J. Braverman

Printed in the United States of America by Cottrell Printing Company

www.3taospress.com

For our families~

Michele, Alicia, Russell, Desanka, Grey, and Rowan

Herbert, Gladys, William E., William D., William A., Adelina, Graham, Sara, and Wolf

In special memory of Edith and Dorothy

And in loving memory of: Bradley Joseph Braverman

Table of Contents

Memory Seekers

Every Artifact a Museum

Voyage to the True Self

Conversations: The Nature of Spirit and Matter

Preface

Collecting Life began with a conversation among writers. Over wine and tapas at the historic Taos Inn, it was a time to celebrate a successful poetry reading and to relax with the kind of small talk that leads down winding side roads, personal and poetical. Unexpectedly, the subject of collecting came up. How surprising that we all had secret lives as collectors! Soon we were immersed in stories about what we collect, when we began, how we have hunted for those objects of desire, and to what lengths we were willing to go for them.

For one author, buttons were her obsession. Yes, buttons. The antique ones that adorned her western jacket. One of us asked where she'd found them. "Every poetry reading. Every conference. Every trip, I haunt antique stores and flea markets. But I'm the black sheep of the button community: I'd rather wear them than keep them under plastic." We raised a toast to a rebellion that took collecting out of dark cases, even if the buttons eventually lost their shine. Another poet reached into her pocket, placing a silver oval engraved with the word *serenity* near her plate. She followed it with an owl charm and amber prayer beads—talismans triggering more life tales through the lens of collecting. Isn't this always the way?

For Madelyn, it was the memory of attending auctions at age five with her grandmother. She remembered holding up the paddle, the auctioneer's staccato refrain, the thrill of winning the prize, even the start of her first collection—perfume bottles. For Andrea, it began with her parents, searching stores in lower Manhattan for silver teapots and French porcelain. Most of all, she was fascinated by the oil paintings on the walls, forming stories, then poems, concerning the stern portraits of strangers.

On the way home that night in the car, we wondered how many poets had written on the theme of collecting. Neither of us could think of a favorite poem about it; neither of us could name one of our own. Madelyn laughed that although she had a private collection of close to a thousand volumes of poetry, not one touched on the theme of collecting.

Over the months, we expanded our conversation to include friends and colleagues. We did not find anyone who does not collect something—from the simple and ordinary, such as matchbook covers and seashells, to valuable collections of artwork currently on loan to museums. There were collecting buffs searching for the expected—toys to recall their childhood or arrowheads to remind them of what has been lost. And who doesn't have a refrigerator magnet or two? The unexpected was just that: reels of B movies. Worms. Riddles. Handcuffs. Whale sounds. The universe of collecting expanded exponentially and was infinite.

If no anthology about collecting existed, *why not,* we asked ourselves. And why couldn't we be the collectors of such poems?

Challenged by the question, we researched articles, literary journals, and a wide range of other media on the topic. Yes, we did discover a poem here and there on collecting, but we quickly realized that we would have to commission poems for a book. We advertised in *Poets & Writers,* designed and sent post cards to poets we knew and poets we wanted to know. Thanks to writers such as Denise Duhamel, Christopher Buckley, and Scott Wiggerman—who solicited collectors, encouraged MFA students, and spread the word—our mailbox box began to spill over. Poems arrived from as close as Colorado and New Mexico and as far away as France and the Solomon Islands, poems from established and emerging poets, experimental and formalist, from inside and outside the academic world.

As poet-ethnologists we began to group the poems into traditional categories—decorative, metaphysical, scientific, sacred, and cultural—but we also were attracted by those poems which went beyond description to insight about the complexity of the human need, which some call *madness*, to acquire, to accumulate, to organize, to display.

Collecting clouds, Mao buttons, even a bottle of teeth served as springboards for reflection. How does poet John Fitzgerald, in his poem, "Creation", teach his son Schmidt about life? Selecting from jars of seeds, he pours water over a single bean cradled in his son's tiny palm; together they watch as it begins to sprout. In "Swinburne Island", Kimiko Hahn considers how "we collect what we collect with varying intent", writing of a young ornithologist who examines "cormorant vomit" for what it contains. Continuing, she notes that we "flaunt what's been consumed:/Grandma Ida's wienerschnitzel. Uncle Jack's Sunday comics./Auntie Kimiye's pearls..." because we are what we consume.

David Trinidad, in "Ode to Fluff", humorously examines Mattel's line of Barbie dolls via persona. When he writes, "O Fluff, no one knows who you are" and "In essence, Fluff, you flopped...", he concedes the doll is not considered worth a great deal. But, still, the speaker sees Fluff's value in kinship: "O smudged kid! O angry loner." And what could be more delightful than Alexander Lumans' narration of an armadillo hiding Valentine's Day cards to be discovered later, or not! In this narrative of family tradition, the poet moves beyond the past to observe: "See: what I remember most is what is never found."

We would be remiss if we did not remark on an unusual category unique to this book—words. Wendy Drexler insists that the formation of words is an important element in our understanding of the beginning of the world: "After our clay dried and hardened,/words were a broth and our tongues/stiff ladles… ." CB Follett writes of an early mentor who values language so much, "She has been out gathering words,/her pleasure and the spine of her life." And so, too, the poet for whom words are sustenance.

After we reviewed the themes of the poems, one name came to mind as the person best qualified to contextualize the subject matter: Bill Brown, Karla Scherer Distinguished Service Professor in American Culture, University of Chicago, a noted expert on the anthropology of collecting. We are honored that this scholar agreed to write the Introduction, placing the poems in historical, philosophical, and cultural perspectives.

Ultimately, *Collecting Life* is a poetry book, first and foremost. It was our intention that it address collecting as only the poet can—through beauty of language and economy of expression. It is an ode to metaphor and imagery, which for the poet rings truer than a price list or bill of sale. It is a book that invites readers to experience an epiphany that reveals everything.

Introduction

The Poetics of Accumulation

A middle-aged man finds a piece of beach glass deep in the sand, he brings it home, and he soon finds himself mesmerized by the object itself and wholly "consumed" by a new "ambition": the ambition to secure another object for the mantle that might transform his find into some originating moment, the origin of some new cosmos—a collection. John's collecting habit, in Virginia Woolf's "Solid Objects," strikes his friend as pathological. Fabricating one world means leaving another behind. Abandoning a "brilliant career" and suffering "fatigue and derision," he scours London ("all alleys" and the "spaces between walls") in the effort to find some form (made of "anything—china, glass, amber, rock, marble") that will genuinely enrich his small display.[1]

This story can be read as an allegory of the new value system imposed by the material scarcities of WW I.[2] It more simply testifies to the long-standing interest that novelists have had in collectors—from Balzac's Sylvain Pons and Henry James's Gilbert Osmond, to Bruce Chadwick's Utz and Myla Goldberg's Miriam. And yet, however successful narrative prose fiction has been in recounting the fancies, fortitude, and uneven fate of collectors, the act of collecting would seem to transcend the prosaic; "through collecting," Jean Baudrillard argues, "the everyday prose of objects is transformed into poetry."[3] The claim sounds commonsensical. This is because lyric poetry seems to enact the very dynamics of collecting, recomposing observations and passing sensations within a frame that somehow renders them complete. From the Psalmic catalogues to Octavio Paz's tribute to Joseph Cornell (translated by Elizabeth Bishop as "Objects and Apparitions"), it is clear that poetry is a mode of collecting and a means of paying tribute to both the practice and its products: "Marbles, buttons, thimbles, dice,/pins, stamps, and glass beads:/tales of the time."[4]

---

[1] Virginia Woolf, "Solid Objects," in *Haunted House and Other Stories*, ed. Leonard Woolf (New York: Harcourt, Brace, 1944), pp. 82-85.

[2] Bill Brown, "The Secret Life of Things (Virginia Woolf and the Matter of Modernism)," *Modernism and Modernity* 6.2 (1999): 1-28.

[3] Jean Baudrillard, *The System of Objects*, trans. James Benedict (London: Verso, 1996), p. 87.

[4] Elizabeth Bishop, *The Complete Poems 1927-1979* (New York: Farrar, Straus and Giroux, 1984), p. 265.

Thus a collection of poetry about collecting—*Collecting Life*—promises to disclose the poetics of collecting as such (what Baudrillard calls a "marginal system" wherein "the subject strives to construct a world, a private totality") and to dramatize an impulse that lies at the heart of lyric verse.[5] This collection lives up to that promise. The range of pursuits ("Starting a Plastic Menagerie," "Cloud Collecting," "Word Gathering"), the assortment of objects ("Mao Buttons," "Dachau Stone," "Fluff"), the array of scenes (the "Corning Museum of Glass," the "Beach," the "Arts Fundraiser")—these produce a kaleidoscopic effect, the ordinary crystallized into the extraordinary, the distant transformed into the proximate, the intimate. This collection of poems shows (comically and tragically, critically and empathetically) what is at stake in our contemporary culture where almost any object (hair pins, bottles, stuffed animals) can be coded a "collectible," and where, as Kristin Camitta Zimet writes, "Everyone I know is collecting… ." These writers help us to feel what "everyone" is longing for: "She/wants to lie in the coolness of a map drawer…" (Lyn Lifshin). They document inexplicable attractions: "She lifts one pebble, another,/into her pocket./From time to time takes them out again and looks" (Jane Hirshfield). They recognize, too, what collecing cannot accomplish: "As if collection/could deliver/composure" (W. K. Buckley).

Hannah Arendt argued that we maintain our identity foremost in relation to concrete objects. The "things of the world have the function of stabilizing human life," she wrote, "and their objectivity lies in the fact that…men, their ever-changing nature notwithstanding, can retrieve their sameness, that is, their identity, by being related to the same chair and the same table."[6] But most things of this world—the food and clothes and computers and cars—are eminently consumable, fungible, disposable; far from interrupting the transience of our lives, they illustrate ephemerality at its most banal. This is why Arendt distinguishes between labor and work, between human effort that disappears without a trace and that which results in reification, some more enduring product, a material externalization of human will. Collecting is *work* that arrests the laws of obsolescence and decay, suspending ephemeral objects and incidents outside of time, as it were. In that suspension the collector both confers and derives stability, however real or imagined.

Which is to argue that although collecting is relentlessly spatial—a dislocation of objects, a recontextualization of them—the intended effect is temporal. "I assembled a shadowbox/of things you had touched," Sharon Foley writes. Quinton Hallett records the simple effort to maintain the presence of the past:

---

[5] Baudrillard, p. 86.

[6] Hannah Arendt, *The Human Condition* (Chicago: University of Chicago Press, 1958), p. 137.

Every small lidded box in her house contains

something she's saved from a lost

encounter: sea urchin spine,

dental gold, eucalyptus pods, a fallen pearl.

Peter Cooley recognizes his own unrealizable ambition: "I was practicing immortality. . . /. . . all the rooms of our small house/draped or arranged around my sacred relics." Collecting testifies to the simple anguish of living in the temporal dimension: "I wanted to invent a record,/one worth filing in a historical museum/ of the future age" (Jeanne Marie Beaumont).

And yet, of course, collecting life requires the passing of time. The point is not just that collections, as William James put it in his *Principles of Psychology* (1890), "become, with different degrees of intimacy, part of our empirical selves."[7] The point is rather that, over time, collections can extend the self—can enable a kind of rejuvenation. For what he called the "real collector," Walter Benjamin believed that "ownership is the most intimate relationship that one can have to things. Not that they come alive in him; it is he who lives in them."[8] Andrea L. Watson documents the self's production of the self:

la tehuana constructs her shrine

of perfect self:

7 silver bracelets

hammered tin mirror

barrette with stones of tanzanite

ceramic vase of golden brushes . . . .

Karla Linn Merrifield can see how "in collecting them, these solid stories of the Earth/ remind me who I am on a Sunday morning… ."

But the lives collected in this volume include the lives of the objects themselves, animated not least by the incantatory, re-creative power of the list: "…box top, book,/ Rhinoceros head/fossil, thimble, small and/larger gods, spoons, bottle caps,/keys, hours badly spent, cities…" (Veronica Golos). "You are seldom aware," Rilke wrote in 1907, "that you still need things which, like the things of your childhood, expect your confidence, your affection, your devotion. How does this happen? How does it

---

[7] William James, *The Principles of Psychology* (Cambridge, Mass.: Harvard University Press, 1984), p. 281.

[8] Walter Benjamin, "Unpacking My Library," trans. Harry Zohn, *Selected Writings Volume 2: 1927-1934* (Cambridge, Mass.: Harvard University Press, 1999), p. 492.

come about at all that things are related to us?"[9] For Rilke, among other poets and artists, what we call modernity (or, later, postmodernity) threatens the relationship between persons and things, but of course the earth itself can be unkind to worldly form—

...those unclaimed
fragments of glass

orphaned on the strand,
the ones the tide
unmothers,

those pieces unseen
by passers-by...

Wayne Lee goes on to write, "these are the gifts/for the modest, the/partners of sand... ." Veronica Golos, in "The Collector," insists that

You
are the
Savior of
the neglected,
the endangered, lost
object. They speak to you:
here, here, here is another
only you can find it . . .

Of course, more forcefully, it may be the poet rather than the *collector*—or, indeed, the poet as collector—who saves endangered objects, who brings them into visibility, legibility, audibility by naming them *there* on the page. There, words themselves appear as objects preserved: "...mine are packed and ready to survive" (Scott Wiggerman). Collecting may be a "marginal system," but *Collecting Life* shows how it is life-preserving work performed at the very center of our selves.

Bill Brown
University of Chicago

---

[9] Rainer Maria Rilke, *Where Silence Reigns,* trans. G. Craig Huston (New York: New Directions, 1978), p. 132.

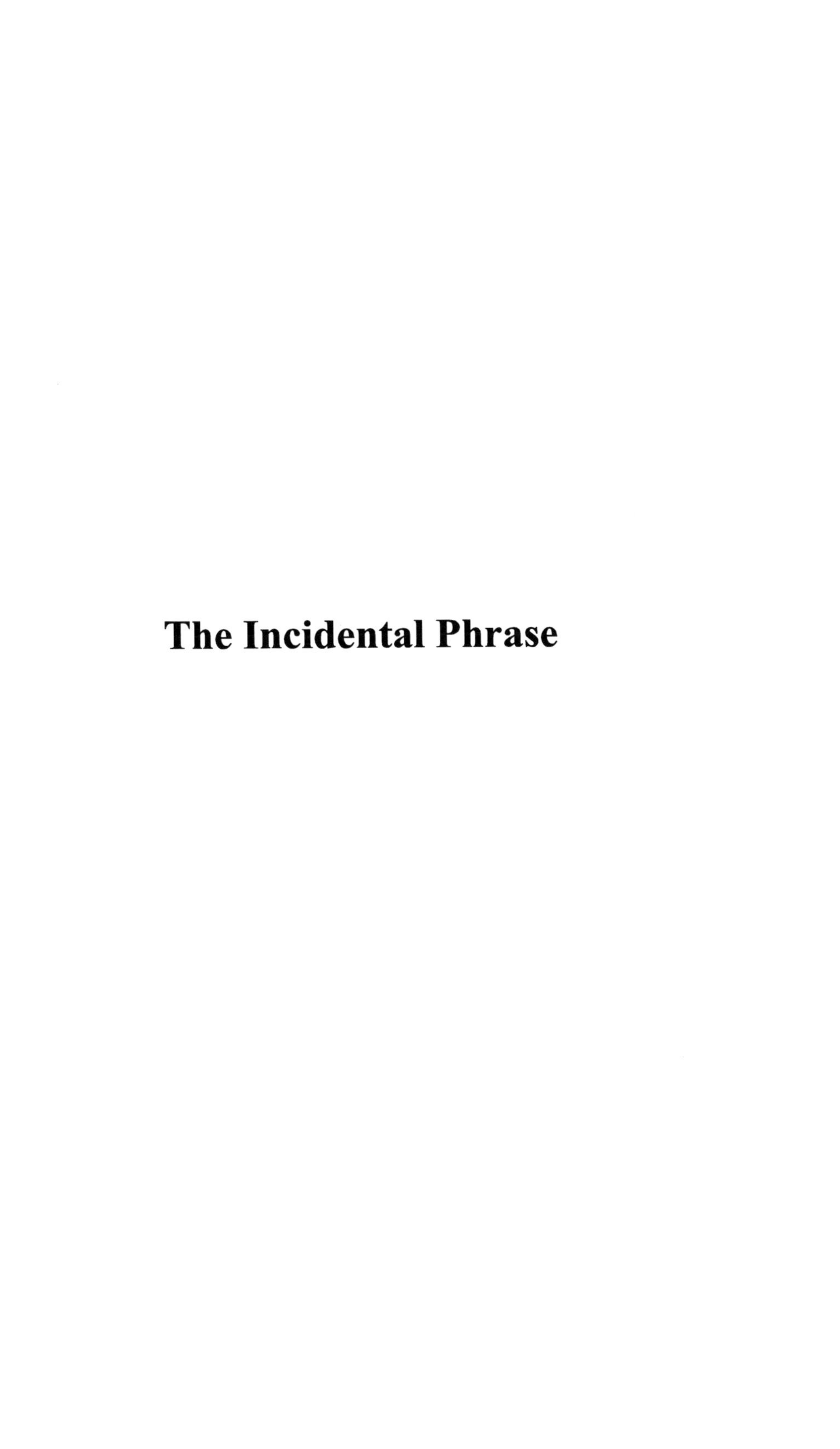

The Incidental Phrase

ADAM

Iconic amid all creation—saw-toothed
palms, the fronds of figs, cooing.

After our clay dried and hardened,
words were a broth and our tongues

stiff ladles—collecting rhinoceros, platypus,
and clattering mosquito, swift, lark,

whale, lithe lynx, moth—until we ran out
of names and describing began—*glittering,*

glistening, flapping, swarming,
entreating. Beaks, toes, even nails

of toes, stretching ourselves thin: *ant, an, a.*

ONE-A-DAY PLUS IRON

Language...comes from everywhere at once. You touch
me all over at the same time. In all senses.
Why only one song, one speech, one text at a time?
-Luce Irigaray

i.
You taught me to read. The first word
of so many, on your lap leaning back
against you, my heels lightly banging your shins,
ankles tangled in folds of your skirt

and suddenly bolting forward bending over
the rounded black letters printed on a plain manila card:

CAT

The pack of cards kept rubber banded, bound
wound round and round, I loved the color of the cards:
manila vanilla One word to a card,
you kept them in an upper kitchen cupboard
bound round with a red rubber band.

Like a gambler, an addict, a thief, I snuck a chair
close to the countertop, climbed.

You caught me—my small hands
wrapped with rubber band
greedily tasting word after word:

HAT MAT SHE EAT TAKE TELL

SEE GIRL I EYE

RUN RED FIND GO COME STOP MORE

LAP LIP HOT COOL DOOR—

“Only one a day for now,” you said, setting them one shelf higher.

ii.
I never dreamed they were everywhere around me: Yield Idylwild Drive
Los Gatos Santa Cruz Aspirin Thunderbird MERGE Marlboro
McCarthy Made in Taiwan This Side Up Summit Road

and in me: *possible yellow willowsway birdtangle songshoes*
creekpaddle splash tomorrow yes yes yes skinsong
purple bloom baby branch waiting for a name

Your voice opening language to me: dry cereal rushing
whisperwheat pillowgravel into a bowl oatmeal spooned in
and swallowed word by word sound of the letters milk
poured *whitesplash* and drunk *drunk drunk*
and satisfying your voice
around words reading to me: read *reed,*
read *red* in the long afternoon
shifting dapplepattern pebbled shadows awake from my nap
your arms around me:
your voice is the voice of poetry, of blood *ironred thrum rusting leafsweep*
rustling that sings through me, taste of crisp words
printed on manila cards.

iii.
And your safe skirt—
my face buried beside your thigh
pulling the soft tan-striped folds around my cheeks
  my eyes my voiceless voice
as you answered the door: GO COME STOP MORE DOOR OPEN SHINE

warmth of my own breath dampening
the fabric *cottonsoft sheetworn* scent of you of me
of hiding your hand on my head fingers hair *tanglesort*

your voice pouring out the door everything at stake
out into streaming light *steam sheen shy shine* into morning air
mourning air dare stare skindrink wind of the world that would
(and would not) be mine—

LOOK BOOK SAY SEE TELL PLAY

NOW MORE HERE HEAR

GREEN SUN BARK DARK MAKE TAKE

AND AND *AND*

THE DUST COLLECTOR CONSIDERS FLY-FISHING FOR SHARKS

Others count, but she sees
numbers and letters in gaudy patterns,
spends her days staring at the sea,
her nights in the arms of a spiral galaxy
then savors the moment of waking and not knowing
who or where she is.
She wants to shed lines of the past,
feel scraped clean.
Sometimes safety is unbearable, she reminds
herself as she sees *Fly-Fishing For Sharks*
collecting dust on the lower shelf
or a 7-inch barbed lure on the top shelf of
PawPaw's beach house,
promise left from a life no longer lived.
Her fortune cookie said not: *A windfall;*
but: *There is time enough to take*
a different path; so she's fishing among
pools of letters and numbers,
trying to string them
into a daring message for tomorrow.

THE WORDS I CARRY

They have traveled notebook to notebook,
emblazoned from far-flung destinations
like stickers on a portmanteau: *bracken,*
hunger, iguana, totter, reverie.

Some have come from dreams: *wingbeat, undersong.*
Others seem a witch's incantation:
fizzle, stipple, indigo, hiss.
Some are short and sharp—*scuff, blunt, shard—*
while others are the soft *wisps* of *whispers.*

I'm a sucker for sibilants,
a lover of laterals,
and when the two come together—
luminous, elicit, delicacy—
I add them to my itinerary.

I'm drawn to islands of *i's—precipice, frivolity—*
and wide-mouthed coves of *o's—billow, froth, frisson.*
I know my *proclivities.*

If I had only moments to save a handful of words,
mine are packed and ready to survive.
I would repeat the words I've collected,
speak their syllables *gingerly,*
track their *incandescent* magic
to any port of call.

WORD GATHERING

for Ellery Who Loves Verbs

She comes, an old woman
with the eyes of a kestrel

and her pin feathers are dappled
when she spreads her wings.

She has been out gathering words,
her pleasure and the spine of her life.

They hold her bones together with a minimum
of rattles. What else could she ask for?

In the rain, words have been easy
to find, settled like leaves along the path,

and besides, the more experienced nouns
know the old woman will be along.

Today she is looking for verbs, strong
with youth and blunt as hammers.

She'll gather them in armloads
and carry them off in her cloak.

The woods are full of adjectives. She loves
their sounds, their bright lifting colors,

spends long hours admiring
their rolling descriptions, but the old woman

serves the poets, who have less use
for adjectives, seductive as they are.

When the poets come,
they jostle each other looking for words

both exact and new,
scoop huge piles and escape with them trailing.

Unchosen words rustle
around the old woman, nudging

her shoes, her hair, as she assures them
other poets will come.

WHAT CAN BE DONE WITH WORDS

Words are more plentiful on the way out of the city where shoes don't make noise as they wander through life longing for each other, scraping their toes against the aggregate; where breath, strangely unwasted, exhales in crowns of amber spikes; where disguise is possible and contentment has legs, emerging bruised but restored from short pants, confident in the direction of the path. Clarity is their reward, like a quilt of steaming eucalyptus leaves delivering steady whiffs of solace to the lungs and throat. Everything is made of silence. That is the secret of words.

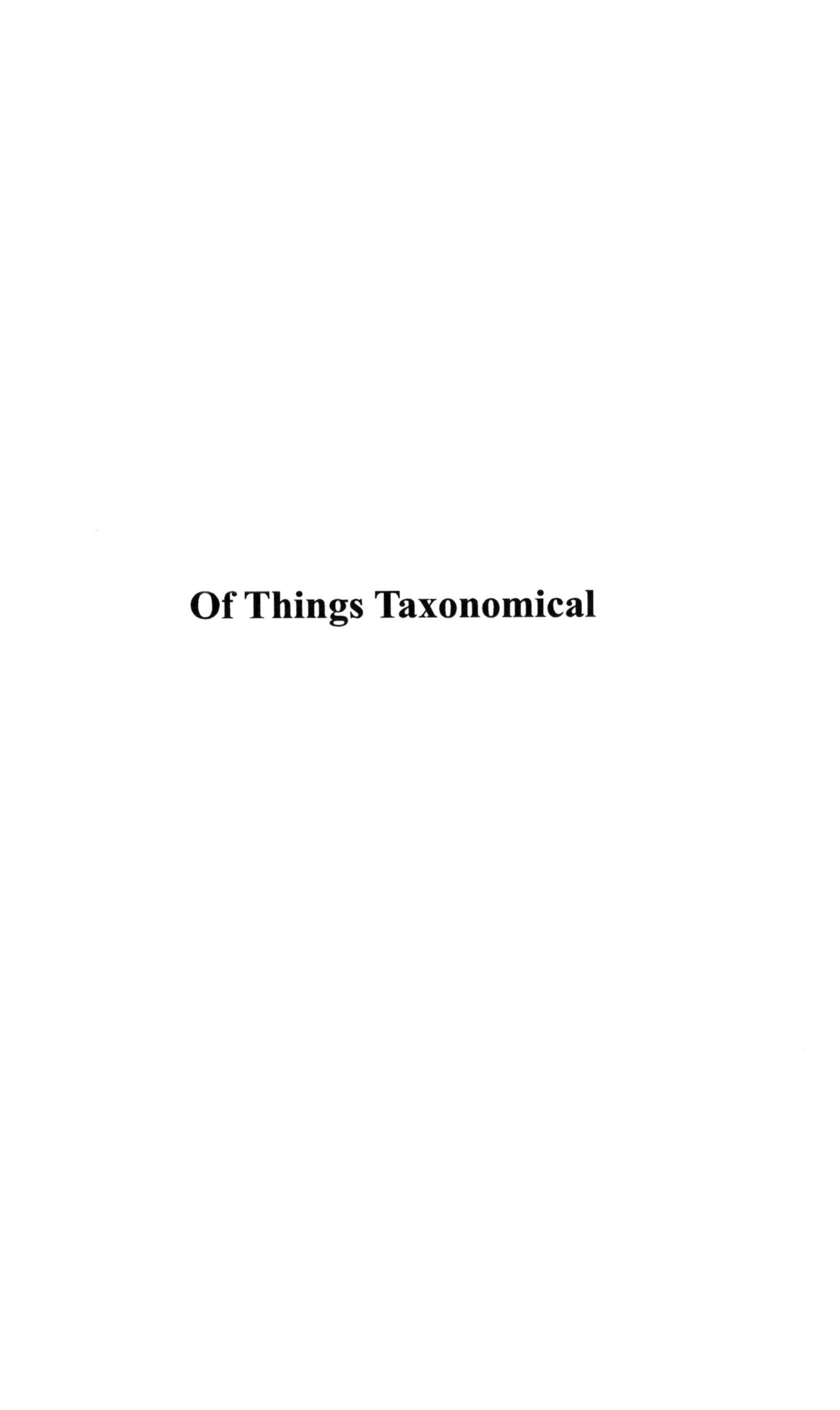

Of Things Taxonomical

THE COMPOSER, THE BONE YARD

Across my work yard the bones lie,
a rubble in crests and waves, piled
white, grooved brown, ocean to ocean—
dirt, ash, bevel, hovel. The rib staves
maintain their swell like breath held.
Fetal vestiges curl, dead in their dead
pelvis bowls, hard seeds stopped
in fossil blossoms, pearl stones
in cracked shells.

I dig and scrape, horizon
to horizon, unearth, unheaven,
fasten and hinge great saber tusks
and broken mandibles, tiny notches
smaller than dormouse fang,
titmouse toe. I latch and lock
together the fractured pieces—ball,
joint, hammer—sew and seam
with brass threads, fit pegs
into their corresponding jigsaw
hooks, count my knotted strings
and bands. I untangle, match,
mend, lathe the past-to-come
in this graveyard where I work.

Sometimes I think I feel the splintered
herds beginning to emerge whole
and in motion, the fallen flocks
to sound and wing. Perhaps I see
dry fish skeletons come weaving
out of rock to water. Resurrection
is my work and belief my resurrection.

The composing pattern of these bones
is the only world I possess, the myth
of my eye, the measure of my ear,
the defined day of the definition to be
when finally fully assembled I can rise,
shaking off dust and rain, roaring
many-voiced, many bodied, and raucous
with new hungers.

MORPHO

I want to meet the man who named the butterflies:
        the *ulysses butterfly*
        the *morpho patroclus*
        the *graphium agamemnon with neon spots.*

Or maybe it was a woman, alone each night in her tent
in the wild, no man but Homer safe to take to bed.

Yes, I'm sure it was a woman.

        "The *ulysses butterfly* feeds on lantana flowers
        and can be lured by blue cloth waved in the air."

When I find my butterfly expert in her lilac smock,
I will uncork a bottle of nectar. We will drink

to the *banded morpho patroclus* who is often tipsy
on fermented fruit and therefore wobbles in the air.

We will take turns sipping from the same chipped cup
knowing we both know how to be patient,

knowing how Helen on the walls of Troy
lifted her breasts like brilliant high fruit,

and how our own stretchmarks and scars
turn iridescent along the ancient trade routes.

LAUDS

Greeting the day
name by name,
buckeye, paw-paw
magnolia, and *bloodroot,*
the underfoot tangle of *kudzu,*
I wake up. I take notice,

or so my husband says,
the teacher as always,
when we hike these mountains.
He shows me the names
he's collected. *Phacelia.*
Wild Ginger. Grass
of Parnassus. He tells me

how *trillium* swept down
the hillside one morning
like angel wings
(small angels!)
come to rest creekside

where *branch lettuce* waits
every April for Cherokee
fingers to gather it.
He makes me stop dreaming
over the switchbacks
and look down. Or up.

Sarvis. Tulip Tree.
Mountain Ash. Trumpet
Vine. Ringing the bell
of each name, so he goes,
and I follow, the echo
behind him, repeating
each beat of the clapper.

WHITE GLASS

It is that
which generally gets ignored—

the plain, the
pale, the subtle—
always there,

available,
those unclaimed
fragments of glass

orphaned on the strand,
the ones the tide
unmothers,

those pieces unseen
by passers-by,
the dullards

of the diamond clan,
forced to consort
with rocks—

these are the gifts
for the modest, the
partners of sand,

this is the sun
melting like desire
for the bride of light.

ON THE BEACH

Uncountable tiny pebbles
of many colors.

Broken seashells mixed in with whole ones.

Sand dollars, shattered and whole,
the half-gone wing of a gull.

Changed glass
that is like the heart after much pain.
The empty shell of a crab.

A child moves alone in the grey
that is half-fog, half wind-blown ocean.

She lifts one pebble, another,
into her pocket.
From time to time takes them out again and looks.

These few and only these. How many? Why?

The waves continue their work of breaking
then rounding the edges.

I would speak to her if I could,
but across the distance what would she hear?
Ocean and ocean. Cry of a fish.

Walk slowly now, small soul, by the edge
of the water. Choose carefully
all you are going to lose, though any of it would do.

NAMING SHELLS

Dusk spreads through leafless maples, turns trunks
into gray columns holding up the sky.
Not candy, my father says,
pressing the paper bag to my palm. On payday Fridays,
he would buy the moon for me,
wrapped in boreal curtains
sprinkled in cardamom and ginger if he could. Instead, trinkets

from Woolworth's; peppermint sticks
like barber poles he saw as a boy.
This time, his favorite shell
to start our collection. Along the strand at Carr's Beach
or Sparrow's or Sea Gulls'—
wherever Sunday School picnics
for its summer outing—we stuff

our pockets with others we unsand—
mussels, clams, snails, conchs, oysters,

sand dollars, sea stars—which swim home
up the Chesapeake Bay when my mother tires of clutter
collecting dust in our bungalow
until shells and bungalows alike
fade into anecdote.

Tonight, a halo rings the moon
as snow drifts over my house. On the book shelf
in the back room,
in a reed basket my mother wove,
the shell she calls a cowrie; my father calls a tiger.

SWINBURNE ISLAND

for E

We collect what we collect with varying intent:
mammy dolls, corsets, scrip,
gall wasps, and for a fledgling ornithologist,

cormorant vomit, or what his advisor describes as
frantic ichthyology—a search for ear bones or other fragments
that could identify a certain species among the partially-digested.

The handsome devil-birds, that dive like penguins
and fly like ducks, are drying their spread wings
when Colin climbs onto some rocks

just below the Verrazano-Narrows. On Swinburne Island
once a quarantine for immigrants, now rubble
the young man sees the birds flushed from thickets

and hears the dumping of stomach contents—
eels, mud snails, oyster toadfish, menhaden
and the common cunner, tautog, and weakfish—

which they do to lighten for take off or signal, *Get lost.*
Or flaunt what's been consumed:
Grandma Ida's wienerschnitzel. Uncle Jack's Sunday comics.

Auntie Kimiye's pearls. Burying a tiny terrier up to its neck
but just for ten minutes. A little sister's blanket.
A thump, smelling of mummified fish remains

and prized by an ambitious graduate student
whose own gut is frantic with fortune, *tangy and rotten.*

ONE HARD LESSON

Cultivating a modest rock garden inside my house,
I scatter stones on shelves and sills
or deposit them in desk and dresser drawers
so I may stumble across them at odd moments.

When I strain for a slim volume on geology,
one by McPhee, a chunk of granite sparkling
with Herkimer diamonds dislodges. Or unrefined
turquoise far from Mexico's Rio Grande is shoved aside

as I wipe dust off the kitchen window ledge.
Smooth, heart-shaped Lockport dolomites line up,
paperweights I have gathered from Lake Ontario's
shoreline fifty feet from my front door.

Fossil-bearing Texas sandstones share a glass bowl
with Alaskan jade and a miscellany of Ordevicians.
Others in a jewelry box are of origins unknown.
Ones I intentionally return to periodically,

when I know I need exposed geologic layers
to mirror the depths within myself, are Vishnu schist,
a scant handful of chips and bits of that most ancient
stone I unearthed near the Colorado River

at the base of the Grand Canyon's inner gorge.
From a worn Ziploc, I release the precious few,
near-black shards on near-white flesh of my palm,
like near timelessness on my curving brief lifeline.

Then I can say all this, see all this, how,
in collecting them, these solid stories of the Earth,
remind me who I am on a Sunday morning,
knowing the destiny of every rock is to become sand.

BOTANICA

My garden spreads across the walls,
each flower numbered, fenced in its frame,
each petal-painted head rising
over an erect green stem
against the lacy outline of a leaf.
Below the stem severed roots
and detached seeds depend
over the names of their creators:
Syd. Edwards, del.; T. Curtis, pub.
No space remains to name the women
hired to paint the petals,
make them live in yellow, purple, red.

When I cultivate my garden, polish
its non-glare glass, I honor the dates
of each flowering: 1818, 1803, 1793, 1791.
Here is no dying. No wilting. No weeds.
As I dust their frames each specimen declares itself—
Tanacetum vulgare, Primula acaulis, Monarda fistulosa—
hanging in its appointed place
as if there'd been no fall.
But that trace of purple outside the line of *Olea Europoea,*
that bare spot on the fruit of *Tamus communis…*
In these slips the spectral hands
of nameless women plant seeds of disorder
in my perfect garden.

ONIONS

It was the year she came to love onions. She couldn't get enough of them…dug them up from the field, slept with them under her pillow, hid in the pantry at night so she could count them. She piled them up in baskets and bins, moving them from one corner to the other. Soon, there was not enough room in the pantry. She carried them out into the living room, organized them by color and shape. The dried outer skins drifted about the floor like spring snow.

She sang to them, checked on them often to make sure they were all right. At night, she held them up to the moon.

The onion lady wandered in and out of the seasons. She squeezed the onions of their milk and rubbed it into her skin. She placed an onion in the hollow underneath each arm, and carried them around like small birds tucked away in their nests.

Next year, she would move into the garden.

IN THE STILL FOREST HEARD FROM FAR AWAY

In the still forest
a noisome bellow
like a bull gator's
a wild grunting sound
heard from far away
each grunter his own

particular timbre
hammering a stob
a short wooden stake
inches in the ground
with a heavy iron
shaft called the roop

drawing it back and
forth over the top
to send vibrations
into the mound
the tremors driving
crawlers to the surface

in trembling droves
swarming en masse
in prompt answer to some
indistinct instinct
escaping earthquakes
to breed or breathe—

split down the middle
one worm becomes two
making either a head
or a tail of it
but species survival
is never a sure thing—

you don't go worming
you don't get to eat.

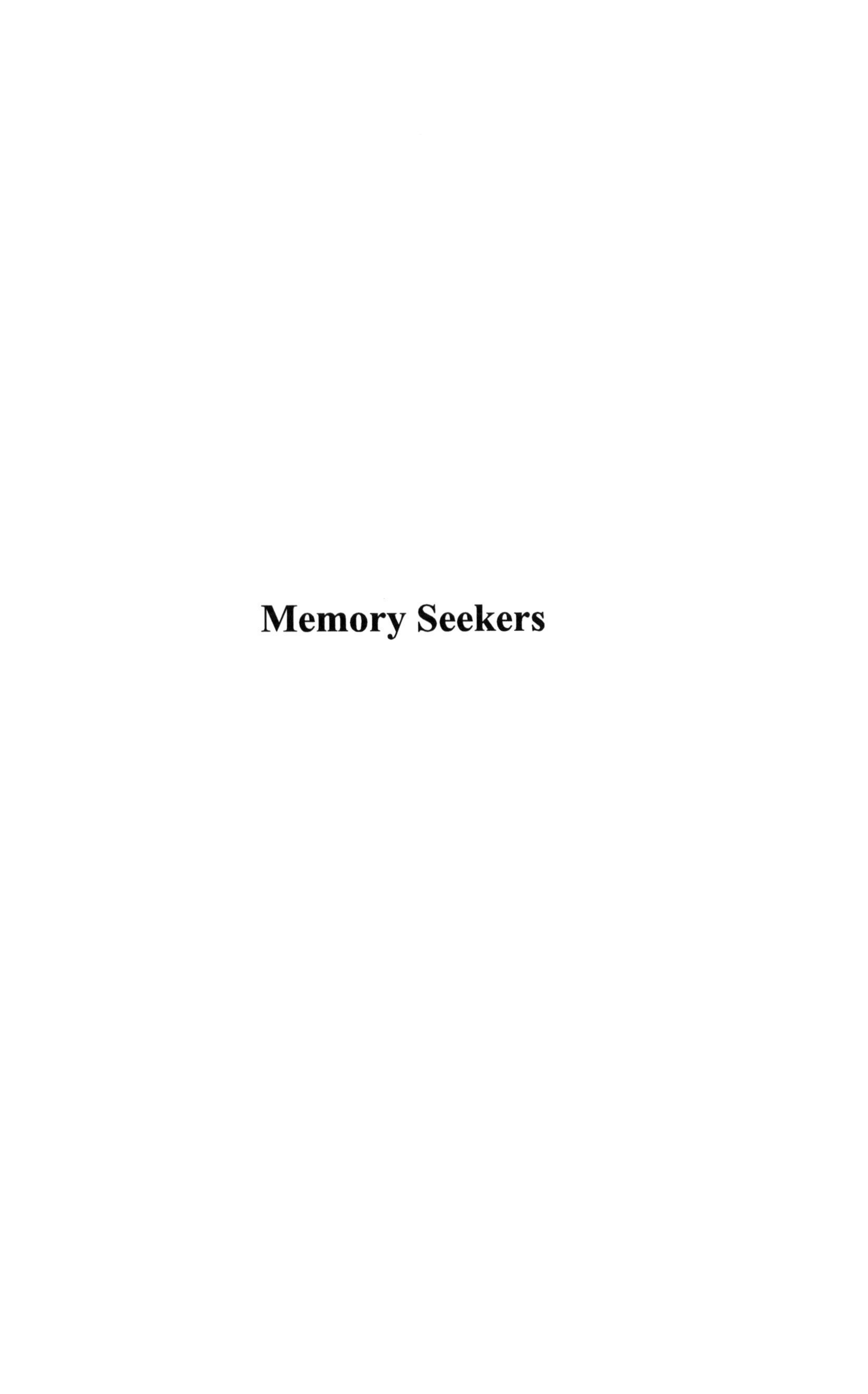

Memory Seekers

TEXTILES

What did I know, what did I know
of love's austere and lonely offices?
-Robert Hayden

We found the bolt of thick purple cloth on the shore
at sunrise—we were always finding things
the ocean had brought in, but never anything like this.
We brought it home, unrolled it through the backyard,
and into the front, like something royal.
It dried quickly in the noonday sun.

Then we swept it free of sand and salt.
We debated whether or not to cut it,
but we'd never get it clean unless we did.
The first layer was marked with tar. We cut it off
and measured the rest in equal parts,
washed, dried, and folded them.

"They'll make such perfect covers,
one for each of you," my father said.
He had been so different that day,
like a small boy having found a treasure.
When he came in to tell us a story that night,
he smoothed our new covers, fingering the cloth.

After he left, I lay thinking of the boy
half a life ago, hiding alone
in the Lausitz forest just east of Dresden.
The fresh rabbit skin as a pillow,
for a cover, the white parachute silk
that had likely floated down the flares before the bombs.

And what he chose to speak about, that time—how soft it was,
like nothing he had ever felt—he said,
it was such beautiful material.

WELLSPRING

She collected waterfalls
Circulated them from the ground
to river to ocean to sky inside her
Five hundred six at final count
Her Blue Ribbon cascading 1450 feet
down Hiʻilawe Falls

The hydro-electric power supplying fuel
for ninety-four years of farm working
square dance calling, accordion playing, art creation
and car tripping with the mannequin Sylvester
napping in the back seat in her dead husband's suit
Hat tilted over imposter eyes

Until she couldn't travel anymore
And the waterfalls plunged
under fingertips on photographs
She scratched off the honey rhubarb
scent of wild calendula
The used litter box fetor of French marigolds
rendered faint by disinfectant of cypress
and ponderosa pines
All of it better than the attic smell of old skin
or urined air in an Alzheimer's ward

Until she couldn't see or smell anymore
But some days the splash and roar of water
still play like old movies
across the cracked walls in her mind
Launching her up and out of the wheelchair
To show her friends in the TV room
how she can still hula
If she holds on tight to the handles
and listens hard for the music

EXCAVATIONS

Across the hill from my parents' house, a woman digging
in her new garden uncovers the fender of a 1925 roadster.

Pouring concrete over the basement's rutted floor,
my parents find milk-crates of tarnished tools,
ancient bottles of wine gone to vinegar,
moth dusted boxes we can't identify,
my baby furniture. Deeper layers unpeel
drums from a drummer my dad hasn't seen since
their days as Kubla Kohen and the Contraband,
playing endless Sundays in the Topanga hills,
Ricky just back from the service and my parents
escaping jobs as county social workers.

The woman keeps digging, hoping for money, finds
copper clay and loam-crusted wine bottles. Her neighbor has
lived on the street since 1932 when the neighborhood was
called *Red Hills* after the communists
raising their rebel children in its shadows. He imagines
the car was moonshine-carrier for the extinct
Prohibition Silver Lake Winery.

Petting his cat good-morning, the old man finds
a dirt-caked replica of the race car
he coveted as a child. My father's band,
now named Red Hill, rehearses, drums and sax
echoing off the hills. Things return.
We never know what we find.

THE ONLY THING I HAVE

And this is how I remember him:
With a business card plus two pictures,
Which I place side by side, next to my own;

With slick black hair, mine curls into question marks.
Thick, full eye brows; a rounded chin like lemon rind;
With lips like cracks creeping into the wall of his mouth,

And a suggested smile, also like mine
—Through eyes dizzied with love
And imperfections.

The similarities melt into something
Undiscovered, unknown.

The card: Mecánico Perito en Reparaciones
De Maquinas de Coser, indicates a life seasoned
By levers, foot controls and the wild buzz

Of needles. The work is guaranteed, unlike the card.
It will never guess it is a broken promise.
It will never know

It is the only thing I have that he has touched.

ALLEGIANCES IN CORA'S ROOM

Even in the States, her room was England
where I was taught to pour from pot and creamer
both at once so the tea wouldn't scald.
Menaced by the false breast that she refused
to wear, I sensed her urgency and learned.

Her closet yielded jars crammed with buttons
for us to inspect. Two onyx cameos
gave audience with Queen Victoria
whom I confused with Queen Elizabeth
and sang with gusto for God to save.

Each stack we made balanced the small change
of lives largely spent, the spoils of family
history hoarded past mortality—
crackled ivories, leads embellished
with velvet, brasses which treasure the light.

The last remnants of brocaded waistcoats
and printed frocks, those tokens paid my fare
on the underground that shuddered
beneath the teeming city of her
eighty years. Her fingers too arthritic

to sew, Cora sorted buttons to keep
accounts, both as abacus and ledger
of her life. And I became her tally
sheet, her auditor, her collateral,
and her currency exchange with time.

THE MINIATURISTS

In memory of painter Donald Evans, 1945-1977

When she showed me the canceled stamps
of Evans' imaginary
countries, their carved postmarks,

I thought how lovely to live in a nation
he named *Stein,*
where, to celebrate the fiftieth anniversary

of *Tender Buttons,* the post office
issued
stamps with quotations from the text.

She lauded his studies of pears, his love
of appearances,
his taxonomies of seashells and palm trees

and took me, first, to fictitious *Nadorp*
for the children's series,
stamps of paired objects, elusive meanings:

bow tie & rabbit; sunrise and comma. Whatever
he loved, he loved
to scale, and then scaled down: an archipelago

of Friends and Lovers (*Amis et Amants*),
or the state
named for the artist *Weisbecker,* in whose loft

he painted the homely *National Chair Works—*
four chairs
in praise of Lower East Side Hospitality.

She embraced her own treasures: World War I
memorabilia, vintage lesbian
pulp fiction, insects in amber, recordings of Caruso.

Preserved like the cat mummy in the British Museum,
the complete handwritten draft
of her dissertation stood in its portable sanctuary.

She'd take it from the tabernacle, part the silk wrapper,
and show me the inscrutable
cross-hatchings, pages smelling of lemonwood.

Over dinner, we enjoyed watercolors of *Mangiare,*
for which he named cities
after Italian dishes and created the region called *Pasta,*

composed of twenty-five provinces, commemorated
on festive stamps
to philatelic standards, properly perforated.

When the affair ended, I walked each day
to the tiny park
with the diminutive swing set and pumped

my enormous feet against the small sky.

THE URN

I tried to save everything
when the cancer mushroomed
and stilled your caved-in chest.

I rifled your drawers
sifted through cupboards,
gathered bottle caps, ribbons and bits,
tickets, strings and papers,
crumpled receipts from pre-washed jeans
and clips from your pinstripe ties.

I assembled a shadowbox
of things you had touched,
a time capsule of discards
until finally I saved
even *you*
inside my porcelain urn.

Tonight I will open the lid
and sprinkle this bed
with your ash,
make a sachet of bone-dust
and rest it beneath my pillow.

HOW HE CAME TO TREASURE HER

Each night he holds her broken
by the rack of cancer,
his fingertips grazing breasts
flat as glass, the fault line of scars.

Steps back into the boy who
treasured marbles he bought to crackle,
slipping heated ladles full
with the ease of a pick-pocket
into the down-shock
and clatter of cold water.

How glorious those globes
teeming with scaffolding,
silver fractures strung along
molecular lines stopped
from entering the universe
by only the thinnest edge of surface

and so fragile that with a single
tap they exploded
into a shower of slivers—
despite his best efforts to keep her whole.

AFTERWORDS

How eager after my parents' deaths
I was to fly them home with me,
cummerbunds of Dad's I swore I'd wear,
Mother's gangrened European jewelry I hung on my wife.
I was practicing immortality, its artifice,
busying myself like a good shopkeeper those first months
inventorying my stuff: all the rooms of our small house
draped or arranged around my sacred relics.
Was it shop, museum or church I was reconstructing?
A golden bowl that could have been James' inspiration
waited on edge for my son's dribble or drop-kick
and a kitsch Greek head from the '30s sneered at me
in my study, announcing poetry could not be written
by a boy as little as the one I was making up
to wander a strange house, searching for his childhood.

I thought when I scavenged their apartment
discarding rusted shoe trees, corsets, three-cent stamps,
I was disposing of the past. That was the first act
in the three-part drama of the Afterdeath.
Part Two is trying on my father's ties,
broad as the tales I was fed of my family's normalcy
in our '50s house; it is stacking ashtrays
from Niagara Falls, Louis something-or-other from France,
another from a Packard dealer (*Ask the man who owns one* on the back)
in the closet since I'm trying to quit smoking
like I'm trying to quit gutting the past
with clutter, when it should be free to be Part Three, memory,
some good, some bad, most ordinary
like my father's giant hand lifting me on his back, Tom Thumb
for a ride or my mother flicking on a blue nightlight
since even today I am afraid to look into the dark
and see how little of me there is to fill the world
then or now, how empty of all of us the world longs to be.

GRANDMA'S GORGEOUS FOSSILIZED BONES

In the gap between pistil and stamen

a faded mauve card embossed with
"I will always love you."

Arranged between lily
and carnation is a hopeful

silence. Shadows twiggy and rich
full of aromatic volatile compounds.

The bushfire clock
extreme, pointy, red

rain on everyone's prayers.
Northerly wind.

Pinned to a doorframe
Casuarinas shed tiny darts.

OF PETRIFIED WOOD, ARROWHEADS, AND DOORWAYS

That toe stubber, door stopper,
colors of a viscous internal organ,
just how my father came by it,
I never learned. I knew he dug up
arrowheads in the creek bed snaking
across our farm; I'd found a few myself,
polished and kept them preserved
in a Mason jar, their points whispering
of jagged wounds, lean winters, war
and the land's irretrievable loss.
The stone wood was more taciturn.
In what field did my father's plough
shake it from centuries' long sleep?
Dropout, he read history, he collected
this tough four or five pound enigma.

Two-thirds of the answer to the first
of Twenty Questions, it stood
resolutely before the kitchen door
in summer, ushering in cherished
evening cool with the gravest dignity.
Sedimentation, intense heat, pressure
say geologists, but I lean towards
Ovidian metamorphosis, a tale warning
us from racing too quickly, urging
careful observation when approaching
and then passing through doorways.
It must still stand somewhere, waiting,
although the makers and finders
of arrowheads have now passed
through nearly all of their doorways.

FROM THE BACK OF THE CLOSET

An empty box; not empty, though: a piece
of earring stuck in a crack where the side
warped clean away; some crumbs. A smear of grease
still holds the ghost of perfume once applied
to neck or wrists; her preference for creams
comes back—less a feeling than a fact—
along with lips, eyes, laugh. A flat light beams
on the old wood, shows patterns still intact
that felt her fingertips, that yielded to
their pressure to fall open and expose
its treasures. One, enfolded neatly in blue,
was a man's gold ring. Whose? Now no one knows.
The top fits snug; the bent silver latch locks.
Go on, put it back now, the empty box.

HOOSIER HISTORIES

More delicate than the historians' are the mapmakers' colors.
-Elizabeth Bishop

Like the guy at the register in the secondhand
shop describing how he was fifteen years into
a five-year remodeling job—*his perennial*
punchline—when his house burned down,

this is the spring we finally get around
to paving the walk with stones gathered
between rains before the neighbor's
corn's too high, pilfering the piles

of rocks children and horses hauled off
a century ago when this cropland was first
cleared by pioneers one generation after
Tecumseh's band was ambushed at nearby

Prophetstown where today the monuments tell
their tall tales of patriotism among the headstones
at Battle Ground: Harrison's men—*who'd have*
imagined him President—who fell at dawn before

burning every kernel of corn. This morning
I come across older stone blades, scrapers
and hand axes that even farm kids wouldn't
recognize—*everyone knows an arrowhead*—

and cleared with the rest: chert that fractures
with a surgical edge, granite so coarse it cuts
by grinding, and quartz too hard to work
that won't ever wear out. Here at the edge

of our fields that yield biodiesel fuel
these days, the stone age sleeps
just beneath the surface, tools
that would still skin a deer—

in the right hands.

SAP GUYS

I drove by your farm this morning, Joe, and saw
steam wafting up from behind the barn,
knew you were boiling. It heartened me to see it.
Had I more time I would have stopped.
As I face divorce, having caught the damned virus
sweeping through town like measles, I wonder
what it is that sends a man out in March
to stand alone for hours in a shed or trudge through
piles of snow or mud lugging heavy, sloppy pails.
Seems all year I've been out in the cold
trudging through slop. You sap guys go to
so much trouble for such little syrup,
but then perhaps you enjoy the trouble,
like a wife. *Bubble, bubble, toil and trouble,*
my wicked friends standing over your caldrons
waiting for the specific gravity to be right
in all the manly science of it, enough sugar
to buoy up your glass stick. You've got
your halved oil drum for a wood box under
the stainless-steel boiling pan your Dad welded.
Then there's the old woodstove from the roadside
Steve rescued and his used restaurant supply store pan.
He stands in the woods of Amherst by his fire
looking like a vagrant. Police cruise by to check him out.
Michael built a shack out of cheap aspen
then shelled out for a real evaporator.
He actually makes some money like a good American.
All this for a little sweetness on taste buds
that disappears like snow on the cheek.
Gets you out of the house I guess, for more sweetness—
the smell of mud and the red-winged blackbird's trill,
proclaiming the small thrill of its life.

TWO MEMORIES

Forty thousand palms bloodied on the handles of pickaxes
chipping ice in northern China, shards lacerating cheeks
stiff with cold, this multitude paving a road
with clay and sand.

Later, sightseers would cruise the highway
snapping photos of vistas serene with the dead,
Soul-Perishing Vale now a grove
where families lunch in the shade.

Pickaxing my way up the Selway trail
half a century since, I stop to drink
from the river, find two arrowheads,
let them lie.

The sky yawns like an open tomb.
As rafters drift past, a sunburned man
spots my tool, lifting a thumb from his fist,
though my palms are not bloody, nor cold.

HOLIDAY LIST

Slowed by snow we finally unlock our peace—
bunker on Cannon Beach, the hue and cry choreography
of work and debt temporarily outdistanced;
Lindenmans bin 65 chalking our mouths like Tums:
iris-scented corks underfoot jammed then released
the accelerator at 85 outside Kalama. We sang maudlin
vaudeville—*Bongo Bongo Bongo, I Don't Want to Set
the World on Fire, Baby It's Cold Outside*—to stay awake
until quaint lanterns illuminated the spit fronting Webb's
Scenic Surf to guide us through the darkening, gull-laden
estuary. Almost Christmas, and so tired Ivory soap and hard
water is a spa; the brown vinyl dorm fridge offers four
of an abandoned Rainier six-pack.

At Port Orford bay, kestrels and gulls screech
over shrimp schools and the offal from fish dressing
stations. Brine-shellacked haystack rocks, sea-blasted
Baked Alaskas featured in so many bad paintings daubed
for tourists, are simply beautiful. Thunder-eggs, spiny grapes
and mauve agates crunch comfortably underfoot; an old Inuit
sells soapstone birds, otters, bears. The stacked crab pots smell
of pepper & ammonia, harshly pleasant with piquant
fir and a dash of diesel as the dim sun photosynthesizes
jackhammer-moss spackle-fattened atop leaky skylights.

The gas-log on Hi dries our sand-caked Nikes
until ancient baseboards hum to life pinging & clacking
like moths in a carriage-lamp. We compare the blue heron's strong
cry to the whooping crane's angelic snicker—twilight music
on the deck of your parent's cabin last spring in Texas—
as we stumble over driftwood on a frigid, moonless Oregon
beach where the surf-lights have burned out & we are nearly
out of money, but in love and on holiday; tonight we celebrate.

HAVE SOME TEA

It pulls me like a rope down into the center of the earth
where I hide and all the while tears go streaming
down my face. My heart a huge purse I dump
all sorts of people in. The girl with the clubfoot
follows slow behind while I walk with her mother.
A boy says how he ran away at fifteen to marry
and so that is how he never finished high school.
He learned how to write bad checks. He was the best in Spokane.
So he only eats shark for breakfast in prison
because he never had a chance. He hates sports cars.
Or my father droning on and on about some water buffalo
from a long time ago and the tapeworm he threw up
in rural China. Boy! It was long he said and I bury
my head in the lagoon seeing nothing. Nada.
Like the Japanese woman in Spokane, who sold all
her rosewood furniture, to leave Japan with her
husband. Maybe that could fill a garbage dump
if only there was a place for it all.
Like the cabaret dancer in Tokyo. I met her
after seeing her Sri Lankan husband on a Kichijoji
train platform, taken by the police away from her yakuza lover.
Back at the American House she makes watery seaweed
soup and some rice and I eat it all in. Her boy and girl smiling
then chasing each other while the diamond dealer
clucks away about his wife dancing with diamonds
while the Tokyo men scream. I grab my purse
and suddenly I'm here in Majuro drinking iced tea.

BEER CAN WRANGLERS

My mother never liked my favorite cousin.
He smoked and spit tobacco and was proud

of living in Lincoln, Nebraska.
He hung his Wranglers on a clothesline

and beat them with a bat.
I wanted to imitate everything that he did.

Wayne was immune to pimples
and spoke with a nasal cornhusker accent,

swung his arms like an ape
until I peed my pants.

At the age of thirteen he owned
the most incredible collection of beer cans

I'd ever seen: flat tops and cone tops
in pyramid stacks.

I couldn't help following him
like some crazy Italian general,

our sacks clinking through
those dingy back-alleys of Detroit.

When we'd finally trudge home,
the screen slamming behind us,

my mother would gasp at the smell,
at the dirt stains on my pants,

then drag me to the bathroom,
into that crash of running water.

WORRY PEOPLE

In their thin oval wood box
the *muñecas quitapenas* are colorful and bent.
With arms in impossible angles,
the little dolls await
a new assignment before bed.

Unburdened of the last affair—
that fragrant reef of duplicity—
onto the *tapados* and *faldas* of the worry people,
the sleeper dreams of conch chowder,
darting parrotfish, a diver
in his sleek skin brushing her arm
at snorkel depth as he swims by.

Who wants to awaken this *soñadora*?
Every small lidded box in her house contains
something she's saved from a lost
encounter: sea urchin spine,
dental gold, eucalyptus pods, a fallen pearl.

If the trapped dolls can work it out
before daylight, let the pearl
and the spine use the dark, too,
fathom by fathom, easing the pain
of a thousand other things that turn up.

MAKING UP FOR LOST TIME

When last I looked is as good
as it gets, as good
as *broken moonlight* or the lost
earrings beneath a flower pot, a once-lost

key too small to fit the gate lock
or the antique roller skate, the lock
on the strong box, the trigger lock within.
When last I looked the doll within

the doll was chipped and cracked
like a ceiling by Giotto, a cracked
cup glued back together by a child
repairing her first broken cup, a child

so used to the magic words, *When last*
I looked, that she's found her mother's earrings, at last.

FLUFF

for Lynn Crosbie

O Fluff, no one knows who you are.
You were produced for one brief year
(nineteen seventy-one) after
Mattel discontinued Scooter,
Barbie's little sister Skipper's
best friend. The toy company feared
the first generation of Bar-
bie consumers, baby boomers
nearing their teens, would disappear
once puberty struck. So you were
invented, a fresh face to lure
the next wave of greedy youngsters,
pink pocketbooks full of gener-
ous allowances or hard-earned
baby-sitting money, to stores
with well-stocked doll departments, where
you were displayed, a wide-eyed, cheer-
ful, puffy-cheeked tomboy, blonde hair
in twin ponytails, wearing your
green, yellow and orange striped over-
alls. You came with a skateboard, per-
fect for cruisin' the park after
school with your pal, Growing Up Skipper.
Mattel executives were sure
that you would be a best-seller,
but your short shelf life was over
almost as soon as it had start-
ed. In essence, Fluff, you flopped. More-
over, today, when collectors
are willing to pay ten dollars
for a pair of Barbie shoes, you're
not worth a lot, even NRFB (Never
Removed From Box). I remember
you, though. As a child, I smeared your

cheeks with grease and slid you under
my girlfriend's orange plastic camper.
Barbie dolls were far too mature
for a girl like me to endure.
But not your flat-chested allure!
O tiny mechanic! The cars
I made you tune up and repair!
The engines you put together!
The windshields you washed, the batter-
ies you changed, tires you filled with air!
After work, you'd smoke a cigar-
ette, then skateboard home in the dark.
O smudged kid! O angry loner!
All my friends think that I'm bizarre
'cause Fluff, no one knows who you are.

TINTIN SAVES THE WORLD

In primary colors,
with faithful dog Snowy in tow,
Tintin rids the globe of
bullies, brigands, and bad guys.

So never mind if my first
boyfriend likes Calculus,
and Captain Haddock needs AA.
So what if the Thompson Twins,

to be precise, are foiled again.
Who cares if from the next room
come shouts, thuds, and thundering
silences. All I know is here

in this room without past or parents,
using wit and wild disguises
Tintin boy reporter saves the world!
My sister and I eat Wimpy burgers

saying, "Trade you *Red Rackham's Treasure*
for *The Secret of the Unicorn,*"
and "Don't get onion ring stains on
my copy of *The Blue Lotus,*"

and I say, "Hergé you're my hero,
won't you fly us to the moon
and maybe just this one time
leave us there."

AT NIGHT, THE VALENTINE ARMADILLO HIDES VALENTINE CARDS

The Armadillo scuttles. Toes tap on hardwood.
Clicks in the night like light switches.
He curls up, balled in dimpled skin with nine identical ridges,
and rolls from the den to the kitchen through the heart of the house.
Someone is listening to thunder.

Card #1: left on the third stair from the bottom, leaning into the shadow.
Card #3: inside the mirror, behind the prescriptions.
Card #12: stuffed between cubes in the removable icebox.
Card #17: left on the floor and matching the shape of tile.
Cards #29 and #32: one in the keyboard, another beneath the mouse.
Each one folded with a perfect name along the crease.

Crawling his way through the house, through the air ducts,
the Armadillo likes coming in through the foil and the dirt.
His eyes see in the dark: everyone asleep.
This is the only home he will ever visit.

See: the glossy gift bags on the porch table.
All four bent at the top, similar to last year's.

Inside: things expected.

Half of the cards will not be found until March, then some in July.

My father will pull his hot sweater from the dryer
to find the outline of a heart melted to the wrist. Card discovered.
See: the unexpected.

See: what I remember most is what is never found.

Every Artifact A Museum

SHOEBOX FILLED WITH MAO BUTTONS

Stubs of sun, deflated saffron orns, scoop up a fistful—
    they chink and clank, megaphones chime *The East is Red.*

Betrothal gifts à la mode, virgin factory girls gave sex
    to comrades, and pinned their souls to Chairman.

Students bartered them for steamy pork buns,
    a professor swallowed two to commit suicide.

Plexi-glass sunflowers, now italicized mementos.
    Dragon-sons, phoenix daughters! Speculate and trade

your shamed nostalgia for museum fortune, Mao on money,
    his mole is art, postmodern aesthetics, the rust is a lie.

Denounce it? Flip one over, needle enjambed,
    hook still kniving, yes, there is blood tinning on your thumb.

BLUE AND WHITE

In a busy city you stopped, and thinking
of me, fingered trinkets, deciding at last on a small

box the clerk suggested could be used to store *cocaine.*

Or dope. Or cocaine. Is it size or beauty
that determines function? Too small to hold a life's

paperwork—the passports, the mortgage,

certificates of birth and death we keep
in the bank's vault—too lovely

for the desk's minutiae of paper clips, transit

tokens, change foreign and domestic, keys whose lost locks
will return the day we purge ourselves of the past.

You apologized for the box's base: not silver,

though just as shiny, malleable tin
embossed with a layered border of flowering

vine. The porcelain cover a shard,

the accompanying statement tells us, of Ming
or Ching vase destroyed by Red Guards.

I've lived through too many revolutions

of my own, been lied to by presidents,
my children, a culture on its way down, to really believe

enough fragments were hoarded for decades

to supply a suddenly available market.
But it doesn't matter if my piece of blue

and white, concave just enough to suggest

the gentle slope of vase neck swelling
into shoulder, is any different than plates of carp

hanging on the yoga studio walls, or the cache pots

grocery crocus spring from, or the teapot thrown
in for a literal song by the bemused secondhand

jeweler, or the collection trundled

onto the estate's grounds for televised assessment.
Nothing's been restored, just made whole

from something broken.

PHOTOGRAPHING THE DOLLS

I wanted to invent a record,
one worth filing in a historical museum
of the future age.
If there was light from the window,
I used that,
or if lamps were lit
lending golden tints of posterity, good, good.

I pursued true illusion—
a recreation where the fake
takes on the psychic heft of the past.
Through each nuance of position: head
tilt, glance sideways,
balance on a half-inch foot
                    —Look, I realize
they might all seem the same to you,
but I was schooled in subtle-
ties, out of fashion at the time as Latin
or home ec, which I skipped.
If you fail
          to be charmed, it
matters little.
For myself I shod them, posed them,
shot them, exposed them.
From me they received books to read,
bouquets, a made bed, dessert.
I hung their walls with paper and pictures
and built them a room. Gave them friends
in abundance, conversations freeze-
framed for their tiny eternity.

Soon, a house. That is, many rooms.
The house made these words.

A QUIETER ART

Even if she were to drop the ball into the Penny Arcade, its roll and plunk would evoke *something's missing*: the time when children made their own toys, training their analytical hands; when children collected ordinary objects, training their aesthetic eyes, the balls of thought running through the brain, *this, no this, that too, and that,* making sense of the world when the world was small enough to make sense of, putting it to order, in boxes and compartments. Until it is as curious as memory. As quiet as missing the dead.

She tried to interview her grandfather for an oral history.

> Did you want to be a farmer? *I was needed on the farm.*
> Tell me about your mother. *She was really nice. She died such a long time ago.*

A room is quieter with a clock in a wooden case, ticking. Reminders. Dividers. Minute hand dusting now further from the dimming past.

AT THE CORNING MUSEUM OF GLASS

first cake baked in glass

In the first exhibit, the scientist's good wife
slits it open proudly in the test kitchen: her cake baked

in a sawed-off battery jar. At the table, her children
smile, toast the invention of the temperature tolerant.

A triangle slice for each: Make your wartime meals
the best you've ever tasted!

I study the children frozen in the photograph while
my daughter slides out of my arms, runs past me down the hall.

*

What keeps each narrative anchored are the facts:

end of layette in a box in a basement
of tiny hospital t-shirts
of socks to fit on a finger
of milk needling through my skin

*

the cookbook holds more than a million recipes for glass

and it is a recipe for language
written by good wife after good wife

Pyrex is best:
add a frit of silicate, sand, soda
and ground lime.

Downstairs I follow my daughter—
behind her, a wake of cries and tantrums and
an assembly line of baby bottles
winds before me like
a long sentence.

*

"Go away," she screams as she buries her head in my lap.

Her body shudders, fists spin against me.
Everything circles around the girl
As we rock together on the cold museum floor.

*

glass dress from the 1893 Chicago Columbian Exposition

another miniature narrative:

They hoped the dress would be
transparent. It wasn't. And it was barely wearable.

Glass fibers break when touched, when the mother
angles the dress over the daughter's shoulders.

Dress of pain the mother put on the daughter.
Dress prickling, needling. Aching dress.

Dress burning the skin every time the daughter moves.

*

then there was the narrative of her first year,
all the while she was becoming:
                    cold spoon I held against her gums for teething
                    milk blistered lips open in sleep

*

glass blowing show

Beside me on the bench, her shoes knock my legs, over and over

while we watch a hot glass river run through with light.

The bubble of glass is iridescent, lit pink, and I remember

watching her as she slept beside me to keep her breathing.

Oh that room lit pink. That baby who is not a baby walking.

And the lesson: not to shatter.

SHIBATA ZESHIN'S *MONKEY POSING AS A COLLECTOR*

Zeshin has made a monkey out of someone here.

Is it the bourgeois patron of the arts
who sees himself redeemed, saved from his lack
of aristocracy by taste, or something like it,
finding his simian true self captured
in delicate, refined shapes of netsuke?

Or does the artist ape himself, mocking
his own ambitions to be lacquerer supreme,
master of artifacts he makes, collects,
and recollects, as all around him old Edo
is roaring toward becoming Tokyo?

Or does he have us in mind, as we stare
at these wittily bizarre reflections,
the deftly arcane musings of Shibata Zeshin,
whose secrets we pretend to fathom,
aping the pose of refined collection?

THE ALTAR OF ONE DARK EYEBROW

in the cracked adobe on martyr's lane
la tehuana constructs her shrine
of perfect self:
                    7 silver bracelets
                    hammered tin mirror
                    barrette with stones of tanzanite
                    ceramic vase of golden brushes
                    hair of the dogheaded god
                    shot glass with worm *y* mezcal

the altar floats from room to studio—
bedroom   herb closet   cocina

always searching for its anointed place:
near the bulto of la Guadalupana? beside

la Virgen's marble arms? on el dia de los muertos
bone dust and beauty decide: el hogar

heat of the kindling calls forth heaven
alignment of luminarias asks for prayer:

may Dieguito remain faithful forever (¡oye!)
may pain of these twisted limbs subside

now lighting of the candles against metal twilight
supplication of milagros quicksilver as her touch

moon like an amulet melting on sky canvas
surrender of the universe to smudge and sage

as shadows embrace santuario of the hearth
Friducha rests beneath firecracker halo of stars

in dreams her right hand paints coral ribbons
and veins   her left hand remembers only flames.

ON A PANEL FROM THE ART CUPBOARD OF PHILIPP HAINHOFER PRESENTED TO GUSTAVUS ADOLPHUS IN 1612

On the architectonics of stone, the billowing accretions
of travertine, an artist has painted his version
of heaven and hell. Dantesque, crimson and cobalt-robed
saints surround the Christ as he sits on a miniature,
translucent crystal sphere. In her star-stitched mantle,
Mary kneels before him, their haloes etched in
gold. Each mineral's layer's limned in a brush-stroke
of white, the rendered clouds puffed as if with
heaven's breath afloat on the hot springs of darkened hell, core
of the crystal, bottom silt of centuries of sin. Like
mottled snails, the castaways, the damned, both feel and stay,
with pinprick gasps, the grotesque devils at their backs.
Fire-tongued and serpent-tailed, the winged marionettes
drive the dead down and down the slender stem of time.

All this from rock sliced thin and polished smooth as shot silk.
The temporal quickened, the drama transformed
into warring factions of good and evil, radiance and ash,
a mystic rehearsal for the dissolution of flesh. *Naturalia*
and *artificialia* contained in a cabinet of myriad wonders, whose
doors swing open and shut, now left, now right:
minerals, corals, stones, and shells, the comely shapes of nature;
apothecary vessels, dark, thin-lipped jars containing
the antidotes of ages, prophylactics to fire the pulse, stay the plague,
elixirs to clear the rubbled corners of the mind.
Heaven and hell anointed on rock, the saintly and the scorned.
Our frailties, foibles, dreams, and expositions
in scarlet lake, viridian, Prussian blue, the milky brilliance
of albumen, a few, delicate brush-strokes on stone.

MEMORY JUG

Earthenware with Plaster and Mixed Media,
U.S., circa 1900, Museum of Fine Arts, Boston

Bristling inside a glass case, a jug—
plaster applied to its outer surface
and things of this world pressed
into the still-wet skin—
embodies *an African-American funerary tradition.*
Oxidized skeleton key, flathead screw,

metal thimble—a hand fixed these
sideways into plaster. Fingers dotted
the surface with buttons, one of tortoise shell,
one baby blue and tiny as a baby's
fingernail, one with raised concentric
rings, and the biggest button, fused glass:

turquoise, gold, cobalt, red, purple.
Not a vessel for ashes but *a grave marker,*
or memorial placed in the home to show, in bits
of one life, articles of passage to the next:
door hinge, belt buckle, miniatures
of corkscrew, scissors, ceramic jug

with finger loop, tilted as though for a sip.
A moon shell, its ear-like interior
exposed, and razor clam shell, concave
side out and leading edge angled
upward, *reflect the African Congo*
belief connecting white shells and rebirth.

PHILATELY

There are smudges now,
beyond the arch behind the display glass,
slate green, pale red, violet brown,
I make out stamps on postal cards

each with a black and white photograph
of a village, its inhabitants
in blacks and whites pose
for a diorama of the villages

blown away at Verdun.
At Verdun in the mausoleum up the hill,
just there beyond the trees,
are the bones of 130,000 unknown men.

I knew this. I had read too
of villages destroyed on this wasteland,
but to leave no stone,
no bit of wall takes my breath.

Here, beyond the arch
in the small white room, colors:
mauve, deep ultramarine,
vermilion, carmine lake and violet.

What remains of nine French villages is here.
Only postal cards
sent before the war by travelers
or cousins visiting from Paris or Metz.

What remains is here.
Beaumont, Bezonveaux, Cumières, Douaumont,
Fleury, Haumont, Louvemont, Ornes and Vaux?
Look for them on a kinder planet.

In this museum of weapons and uniforms,
helmets with and without holes,
Kanon and gas masks,
look under the basement stairs,

through a small arch way that leads
to these rude cards of village life,
(I hadn't meant to stop.)—
in this country that comes easily to mud.

Beside each group of cards
the precise little map of a French surveyor's office
showing where the buildings had been.
L'église, la poste, la boucherie…

DACHAU STONE

Stone from Dachau come to my writingroom
        as gift for me
From woman visiting me who visited Dachau
        and returned with this stone
                she found there,
        just happened to bend over
                and pick up,
Thought I'd find it interesting
        considering deathcamp references
                in my poetry,
"Thought Antler might write a poem
        about it."
On holding a stone from Dachau in Milwaukee,
        I wonder how many poets this instant
                are holding a stone
        from Dachau
                in Milwaukee or the World?
Could be I'm the only one.
Could be I'm the only person on Earth this instant
        contemplating in their hand
                a Dachau stone.
Boot-shaped stone, purple in color,
        on whose sole a ghostly white splotch
                shaped like wraith-like
        winding-sheet
                attached to skull face
        screaming voiceless horrorgape.
Stone from Dachau thousands gassed there walked on,
        their anguished corpses ovened or dumped
                in open mass graves
        making liberators vomit
                and weep uncontrollably.

Stone from Dachau come to Milwaukee chamber
        of Antler in Eternity, into the room
                where he lives and breathes,
        into the secret laboratory
                of visionary sexpoems
        and marijuana hymns written for the utopias
                of 21st Century and beyond.
Stone from that point on Earth of inhumanity's epitome
        come to be shrined beside
                ceremonial wilderness stones
        brought back as talismans
To console citybound me getting stoned
        and placing them on my heart
                or forehead
        remembering the wilds
                where they found me—
That wild freedom and joy
        compared to the suffering and cruelty
                memento'd by this stone.

MY BLOODY ACQUAINTANCES

I just met a Viking yesterday

The Axe Man didn't seem
to be at ease standing
next to the descendants of
Bach, Debussy,
A Mayflower or two,
William the Conqueror,
The Royal Scot and others
with whom I am acquainted,
so I built a new set of shelves
from Organic Ocean-Seasoned boards

His crisp, clever gallery talk
and his beautifully cut
curator's jacket seemed to
fit him much more naturally
than a clunky helmet and hollering,
but nevertheless
blood is blood

and so, a new retrospective collection,
Anonymous Livelihoods,
now resides in the tidy library
in my untidy head,
right down aisle 3D

A LENDING LIBRARY

This is a booke of meteors, as well fiery and ayrie as watry and earthy; by W.F., Doctor in Divinitie.

This book is held together by a rubber band.

This book fell on the head of a girl in Perth, who read it and founded a new school of poetry.

This book irritated Thoth, the Egyptian god of scribes.

This book is a trap door into the underworld, twelve pairs of tattered shoes, and the hapless dozing of young men.

This book has a small wormhole in the bottom margin.

I'm afraid to put this book on top of that book. They both bruise so easily.

This book was made by Wang Jie on behalf of his two parents on the thirteenth of the fourth moon of the ninth year of Xiantong.

This book contains certain grievances.

My secret name for this book: "Mam'selle Fifi."

This book smells like a hot night in a Greek prison and the groin of a voluptuary.

This book was drafted over a long, tempestuous weekend, in crayon.

This is the book not found in her effects, the book not written.

This useful book maps out the hall of looking-glasses, the ogress and the tub of toads.

This pretie one: faint soiling to the vellum. The original gold silk ties.

Voyage to the True Self

FINDING DAISIES

I never dreamt such flowers
not even for a wedding
not even in a dream
of being the florist's daughter
so many
and all at once together
in the same field.

No one told me how daisies
nóiníni
acres of them
grow wild in Ireland.

It was not a memory my people
carried, who gathered so tightly
about them
the dark-eyed flowers
of their own despair.

You laughed, counting one more
of my returned Irish-American
naivetés,
but you stopped the car
and helped me gather
armfuls, dripping at the roots
enough to fill the back seat
and then the boot of the car
and then every vase, every jar
in the house, with their smell,
like iron, or hope.

I ran my fingers over
your great Aunt Bridgie's vase
the finest one, bone china
raised with filigree
and cloisonné, touching there
the edge of a memory
no richer than that
of the bog in my palm.

$500,000

When I was in first grade, I discovered a set of custom pencils in my Christmas stocking. They were the most beautiful gift I'd ever received, all the pencils, red not yellow, with my full name running in gold block letters down the side. I never used them because I had the bad habit of chewing on my No. 2s, and I thought these monogrammed ones were too expensive to wreck with teeth marks. I just couldn't bring myself to twirl one into my pencil sharpener, which would, in turn, churn out curled shavings that looked like apple peels falling into the trash. When would I ever get such a present again? When I went off to college, my parents gave me a Cross pen, this time my name in silver cursive. I kept it in its box, sure I would lose it to a library cubicle or to the bottom of my backpack. *I'll use it when I get my first real job,* I told myself. I used the same compact of blush from 1979-2002, when the brush finally fell apart. I'd brought the blush for my high school prom. Because of my allergies, I never wore much makeup, which seemed like such a wste of money anyway, but even I had to admit 23 years was a long time to hold onto one compact. I reluctantly purchased another one—Clinique—the day my friend Melissa was having her art opening. Melissa was obsessed with Anne Frank and—because Anne had been interested in sewing—made several dresses with labels stitched into them that read "made by Anne Frank." On a table was a scattering of pencils just like I'd received in my stocking, with Anne Frank's name on them instead. The pencils were an eerie symbol of what she would never get to write. Gallery-goers were asked to take them, as Melissa wanted people to continue Anne's story. "Where did you get these?" I asked Melissa. I wondered how she could afford to give them away. "The Lillian Vernon catalogue. That's where I got the labels, too. The pencils were really cheap! Maybe 15 cents each." Melissa's show was a big success—its simplicity, its ethereal impact. The blush, then the pencils led me to search for the Cross pen, since I'd been working fulltime now for over a decade. I had an idea to write about my grandmother, who reused teabags and paper towels, who died having never worn the "good coat" she'd bought years before. Why was she saving that hound's-tooth check? I twisted open my Cross pen, but the ink had dried.

PAPER DOLL GHAZAL

When she was ten, she had a shoebox full of tatty dolls
with painted tag board faces—creased and worn out shabby dolls.

She loved Elizabeth Taylor the most—those violet eyes
and small waist a far cry from her buggy full of chubby dolls.

Kim Novak had a blonde mystique about her quiet face—
sultry in pajamas—ruffled pink paper baby dolls.

Coquettish Debbie Reynolds smiled the widest of them all.
Why not? She hauled in Eddie Fisher—that hunky hubby-doll!

Betty Davis must have been a hand-me-down: the cousins'
boxes of outgrown clothes each fall sometimes held a grubby doll.

When seasons changed, there was no Bloomingdales for paper girls—
no mall—Sears catalog gave hope for all but snobby dolls.

Swimsuits painted on, they couldn't change. But Chris donned a bra
and a cardboard smile stiff as any other unhappy doll's.

REAPPEARING

During intermission, the magician took me aside, showed me to a room he'd recently discovered behind a false wall, turned on the light and said, *Look at this!* as if I would grasp the significance. My blank look prompted him to explain the white rabbits hopping among coins and dollar bills, paper bouquets, and various fake fruits. *When you're first learning the disappearing act,* he said, *you make mistakes. Very common. Turns out it's all a matter of voice—like training a dog—but even so, objects can be stubborn, refuse to return to their vanishing points. Most upsetting to someone who's entrusted you with an heirloom watch or brooch. Imagine my pleasure at recovering such losses!* Now it all made sense—the mound of Boston Red Sox caps, unmatched shoes, sets of keys. And in that cobwebbed corner, the marriage certificate, the gold band, the thin flask of shame.

AQUA ACCELERANDO

That first married year of dinners and leaning to counter
and table top with talk of our days, I began to see

how one could refrain from water, taking juice from fruit,
liquid from a cache of cob-shaved kernels. Consider
the woodrat, euphorically assembling its midden,

and too busy to drink. The nest can last millennia,
the petrified center a record of want. Time slips over

us like silk over silk, like upholsterer's bolts, or bright
swatches spilling from sample boxes. Pick fabrics.

Choose patterns, back-up patterns. Who buys a house
to live in anymore? Choose reds, blend the Victorian
armchair. Mix in cotton when you can. Mingle

false fiber hues with baseboards stripped
and stained. Follow with dizziness, loss of balance.

ONE MORE WOMAN IN LOVE WITH OLD MAPS

finds nothing of interest in revised and accurate Triple
A and Frommer maps, can't imagine a computer
for the dash telling her where she has been, could
be going. She wants a map she can hold in her
hands and stroke like flesh, be like a lover
she can unroll and lie under as if a Persian
carpet, woven of yellows, the bluest blues.
She wants mythical shapes, mysterious as a
woman with a slightly raised skirt you could
spend your life trying to decipher. Color is life,
she hears in a film, longing for washes of
frankincense and ground amber, not a drainage
ditch of a blueprint with nothing that isn't rigid.
She wants maps that are fiction, mysterious
as the carpets nomads spun out of the pain
and joy, sheered the wool from animals they
slept coiled in the warmth of then plunged into
vats of burning poppies, clarets, flame violets
and Jerusalem cherries. Too little in her has
been that raw wool soaking up color. She
wants to lie in the coolness of a map drawer,
wait in darkness for fingers that could smooth
the riot of blood reds, onyx, a trail back to
where something could start again.

REFRACTION

Three glass bottles on a narrow sill.
One cobalt with a fluted neck—bought

after their first kiss. It casts a blue stripe
across the bamboo floor each April afternoon

at three, a light that hits her while she reads,
the hour's silence both quilt and knife.

Another: squat, square and green.
When her father died, she wandered streets

where even dogs hung their heads. She saw
its cloudy lime glint in a store window.

It feels tumbled soft in her hand, as if made
of sea glass, corners sanded by grit.

But the one the color of poppies she loves
and rues—the violin-shaped body—found

on her honeymoon, her future idling
on a runway bordered by lilacs, her marriage

about to take off. How clear it all seemed.
How easy then, her heart nothing like glass.

GARDENER

A stained glass skylight held by
rough hewn beams
sends iris leaves and stems to the floor

in a single ray. On the night stand,
antique green medicine bottles rattle.
We savor cucumber and tea, a pungent

cilantro lingers on our fingers. We've folded
linted linens, blankets, leafy patterned
silks. Our street is lined with maples.

On the neighbor's screen porch sits
a milk glass bowl with swirls
of avocado soft as creamy fruit

kept in a drawer for three days,
safe behind its dark enamel rind.
See the mortar and pestle? I must have it,

and their green tea set, three crystal
etched cups with four matching saucers.
And a lantern with wavy sea-green panes,

depression era plates. I reach
for an emerald green vase
wide enough for one stem, storing a long lost

needle and thread. I want it all,
glass with the whorled drip
of summer lake, the tug of pear skin

giving in to my teeth, that tangy pulp
of artichoke. Green like breeze on my neck
some summer afternoon of melted sand.

Glass pressed or hand blown,
kiln-hot as a hand on my shoulder,
twisting and turning from the fire

like a daughter
delivered, wrapped in orange flames,
then cooling to green.

COLLECTING

Bubbles clustered in blue glass wait for me
to lift a hammer and let the trapped air out.
I enter the lives of objects, lie down
with moonstones that whisper

in velvet-lined cases, join a silversmith's hidden
hoard—coins, dragon cups, heavy spoons.
Lush cloth roses the color of blood,
burnished sauceboats, lipped tureens.

I love mistakes—pitted glaze dripped
from a jar's rough shoulder, straw
stuck to a painting done at the shore.
In one watercolor everyone is flying,

gripping a floating lamppost, a sofa,
an old TV. I'm gauzy, floating wrong side up,
straw hat sailing over my skirts, smelling
the pungent scent of my body, summer long

in its culmination, soft peach light. What if
sorrow let me go? Would I be found,
anxious, world wary, staring into the sun or
floating above the low and terrible painted hills?

PORTRAITURE

I've built portraits with my time
native portraits, rattled portraits
idle and forced that hung like masks
over my more fragile portraits

I've dressed and redressed
my limbs in the necessary chemistry
to give each portrait its ration
of sunlight; I've hid my fledglings

like black teeth beneath my housepillows
praying for magic, practicing my small private
language as the expectation of fluency
printed newspapers in the dark

words that flooded the pavilion
and often broke into sour grain.

*

I've spent my time taking
potent portraits, toxic portraits, make-
shift portraits; portraits that gnawed
at my jaw like parasites

I've folded and unfolded them
to make wrinkles to hide little bits
of hair and bone in those grooves
to remember and forget by

they've been everything
at one time or another—
parables, valentines, diaries
letters, deeds, notes

medicine for sins
dark as roots.

*

I've tried to fathom the nature of these
portraits, how they collect like moths
sequels to what was
never clear

to begin with; I've hung my
arms out like bridges and tried to
analyze the grindstones
we grow from

but never found handles
to make this any easier
I've tried to box the very weather
for later, but

can't resist such
openings.

*

this is the portrait effect
the raw gone raw again
a slight pull making the
reservoir curve just so

an arc of light
rabid and naked; half-translated
but never bronzed; fatal
and fugitive

leaving us with
lesser portraits:

seeded portraits,
shrouded portraits,
riddled and rationed portraits,
quiet portraits;
sleeping portraits.

ROOMS

There is the room in my brain
where I keep dangerous things,
the room where I cheat,
lies sewn together like bearskins,
tanned side down, fur side up.

There is the darkened room in the dorm
where we made out; I thought
ahead for that, chose my underwear,
planned to be surprised.
There is the room where we fought,
the room at the top of the stairs
where I pushed you
and you laughed. That laugh
is a room I left, a door I slammed.

There is the room which was
only a camp cot
where I licked your skin,
soft tongue in the dark,
and there is the empty room
of what you said later.

There is the room, vase-shaped,
where I grew a child
until he filled it and it was too
small for him ever again.

There is the room where my mother died,
drapes hanging in folds as any other day,
sound of mucus in her throat,
sound of my voice
asking a question she will not answer.

There is the room where orchids take shape,
where each one hangs down from a branch
and opens its mute white throat.

THE CHEST

I.

red patent stilettos
black leather push-up bra
lace teddy the weight of a hummingbird
hand cuff key

II.

an unopened Pleasure Pack—3 Twisted
Pleasure, 3 Her Pleasure, 3 Intense Ribbed, 3 Shared
Pleasure—42 love letters scarred with tears bound
by a single black silk sash

III.

a knife
a hatchet
a noose
a needle overflowing with radiator fluid

every single photo I ever
took of you

RARE BLUE MAD BOY

Something to want for no good reason,
like a rare blue mad boy on eBay.
Something you don't know you remember
until you see it, so familiar and strange.

Witch's familiar, a familiar cold.
Familiarity of a gray sky, certain
handwriting and cadence of speech.
You are at home with these things.

You keep going back for more, regardless.
The pleasure of the familiar outweighs
everything else. Because every day
is so damned new.

ON BIDDING UP A RUG ON EBAY

Foxybenmoxy beat me out again, maybe
a decorator or someone
with deep pockets, who bids
huge sums for Afghan, Turkoman, Persian rugs,
like those I bought dirt cheap in September.

Kahuipu and I are email buddies, checking,
comparing, outbidding each other.
With a fast browser, he'll snipe the last second
and burn competition.

Last week, I bid up a Shiraz—let others pay dearly—
made a few bucks for the seller.
Doesn't matter, *Kahuipu* emails me, when he wins it.
I like the rug, but salt bags are still a bargain.

Thanks for the tip, but I haven't got room
for the rugs I own.
Like what would I do with a salt bag?

Why not join *Goaugie, Financy, Mulletspeak,*
Dopeywankanooby, Kahuipu and me?
Bid on a prayer rug—one you don't need—nothing
beats the rush
when *Congratulations* hits the screen.

AT THE ARTS FUNDRAISER

for David Guerrero

Each of their walls is adorned
with the trash of privilege. Here,
gashes of scarlet, dark blues,
and earthtones in the scalloped
force field of a gilt frame; there,
wool that's been dyed and resurrected
as kachinas, turquoise and russet,
splayed upon a warm black sky.
"We collect," the host tells us,
swerving into talk of bond markets
and interest rates.

                              I need a drink,
and quit his company; but return
later with a Southern Comfort
glowing in my fist, and examine
the walls. Glossies of our hostess
hugging Pavarotti (at bottom, a scrawl
reading: "Ciao! *Luciano—*"); another
on the slopes with Billy Kidd;
another on the golf course at Vail,
waving to us all from the arms
of ex-President Ford.

                                    Suddenly
I hear the ice cracking in my glass,
and think: *They collect.* And I see
the good cause that brought me here
obliges me to face such walls, wailing
in silence like a Jew at the Kremlin,
gnawing the bone of my contention,
swallowing words like these.

TRAPPINGS

We're packing up the attic where boxes bulged ten years in mold and dust. They don't contain the gin they advertise. We wish they did. Instead they're full of books we never read, old hats, macramé belts, ceramic bowls we made in seventh grade, misshaped, fragile with pocks. They remind us of what we used to be, which may not be all bad, since even we are not our former selves. Each seven years all skin cells are replaced. Sloughed off with strands of dry hair, and toenails we trim and softly drop, or thoughts shoved through cortex, then lost in our graying bubble wrap. Our teeth, too, yellow, fall out. And sex, that hot commodity, we give with little more than bump and grind. So what's with all the obsolete loot we can't convince ourselves to leave behind? Like this—the box of wind-up toys that terrorized our cool, neurotic cat. Look, the monkey drumming with a stick, the alligator with the snapping jaw, that quirky dog that squats before each flip. Just take the lava lamps and clarinet, bottle rockets, peace signs and rugs. For now, despite what each of us was taught, it's better just to take than give away. Our bodies may have mastered letting go, but even them we'll box some final day. Just in case. Besides you never know.

NAUGHTON'S QUARTERS

Sometimes when I'm walking
in the cemetery
I steal a few
quarters from Naughton

because I need them
for the parking meters
when I'm driving.
This I confide to a friend

over lunch, adding:
Naughton has plenty
and doesn't drive anymore anyway,
and it's not like Naughton's neighbors

notice. Plus his descendents
keep replenishing them—
it must be some kind of tradition,
like placing stones, or flowers—

and then there's the tradition
I'm upholding: the grave-
robber's tradition, the living taking from the dead
what the dead have no need of.

My friend stops chewing.
He looks alarmed, pillaged.
Like he just bit down on something hard
and realized it was his own filling.

Put the quarters back, he says.
The dead have need. They have need.

THE COLLECTION

For a long time you collected the dead,
jay feather, bear claw. Even now in a box,
tail of a squirrel, shell of a snail.

But relics do not interest your son.
He is suspicious. What kind of mother
would want to keep shark's teeth
found long ago in shallow water?
He is alive and running
ahead of you on the mountain.
His dog is his shadow.

September, green going slowly back to yellow,
you want to pick for him one twig of maple,
let him hold one two-colored leaf.
It is too late. He tells you
yellow will come precisely on October 15th,
too many days at a desk, five autumns
with the science teacher
pressing leaves on wax paper.

What can you give the boy this second?
He seems determined to run,
climbing on stones where you cannot follow.
Stop. Wait a minute. No. He turns his back
to you and the spring branch,
diverts his eye from the rock shelf
where thin shells of crawfish gleam underwater.

Leaves argue retirement. Some of them fall
on the path as you walk toward home.
Bones don't know anything, he vows.
You give him your word. You promise
to think more of the living.

ISLA NEGRA

for Pablo Neruda (1904-1973)

Since there's no way of calling up the dead,
I should write you a letter on your gray fence
on the driftwood whale's ribs stuck in the sand
between your house and the old ocean
that laughed to bust its gut to find
itself discovered by discoverers,

stout Cortez, innocent Polynesians, all
the ancient children in my classroom, and you
not first nor last among them, don Pablo,
el Poeta with a capital P, accumulator
of sea-shell spirals, of escaleras secreted
by caracoles thinking of self-armored symmetry,

of wings of jaguar eyes navigating the rain forest,
captains of sails whispered into bottles,
haunting rummage sales and shipwrecks
on every spit and cove of coast
for bare-breasted oaken sopranos that once
cleaved the salt air on a ship's prow,

unpacking gargoyles and virgins,
well-hung ebony icons and the fiery horse
from childhood still exhaling steam
in the farthest corner of the house
forever unfinished as any Inca fortress
with no right angles out of living rock,

rocking as every wave holds its round breath
and kettledrums on granite flecked with shale
past the bar inscribed with the names of the dead
where only you could mix sinister potions
and the hassock stained green with your scribbling
and quilts of seven continents

that drained toward sleep in the only arms
of the woman before that and after that
and the scorpion crawling down into the waves
and the walls of Communism washing out to sea
and what for, señor Poeta, why all this pyramid
of flotsam, museum or mound or house or book

of splendidly attributed trash, if it only
could be read aloud after your voice
was choked with sand, could only be seen
entirely after the jackboots hammered
on the mouths of all your doors,
could only be ignored for all your excess

of sunlight and syntax and splendor
after they carried the waxen figurine
that was your body into a hollow frozen
concrete niche with no more monument
than the name not even yours from birth
and the few remembered flames of flowers?

Here and now, where the final stones of your poems
are smashed forever under the laughing ocean,
I let go of the hands of my own dead,
mother and brother and father and father,
I let them swim away like thoughts.
Accept them, dear Pablo, on your black island.

ESTATE

> *Somewhere the flower of farewell blooms and scatters*
> *ceaselessly its pollen, which we breathe;*
> *even in the winds that reach us first we breathe farewell.*
> -Rainer Maria Rilke

Each piece of paper
each leaf holds
breath left

or scent inhaled
from a piece of clothing
in a green and yellow box
from Brazil that says:

Entrega Urgente
Cuidado Frágil

I spend the weekend
at estate, yard sales trying
to determine if this
is how we measure

our lives, what's left behind
to sell to strangers—the box
marked *free* left untouched,
as though unclean…

In the end does it matter
if the prints of our passing
end up for sale
as rummage?

We sniff the air
inside garages and houses
of strangers, judge them
their lack of taste
their sentiments.

When it is our own,
how reluctantly we part
with these traces—
if we have the choice.

This plastic bag,
the scent its piece of clothing
carries, we are sure we know it
before we seal it up again

In the carton labeled
...Urgent...Fragile.

This scent a breath
still alive
as we take it briefly
into our own
lungs.

Conversations:
The Nature of Spirit and Matter

THE COLLECTOR

First
a thing—
its absence,
then not. Then an-
other…thing wanting
to be owned. A kind
of purpose poured first in-
to the thing which has been select-
ed, carefully, because the thing is needed
not for itself alone but what shines through
it and how it makes its way outward—into
the mind of he who has captured it—and its soul.

Start
with a
figurine
or box top, book,
Rhinoceros head,
fossil, thimble, small and
larger gods, spoons, bottle caps,
keys, hours badly spent, cities,
rivers, whole continents—artifacts
of someone else's life; as if in things
some slippage occurs inside the space within
the space where you feel the itch, and its tick under
your thumb—the scent of its nothingness, a perfume—a soul.

You
are the
Savior of
the neglected,
the endangered, lost
object. They speak to you:
here, here, here is another
only you can find it, the thing—
power—the magic simulacrum
of the past. If only those shadows too
could be coupled with—an umbilical,
this twist inside the gut, spun like a rope
from you to it as if always it was mean to be
(oh), because this pleasure pulls, at the body, at the soul.

First…

CREATION

for my son, Schmidt

I tell my young son, *Watch, I will show you*
the creation of life. He looks at me puzzled.

Before him jars of seeds, seasoned dry
by the harvest sun. Eyes peer from wizened faces.

Black with white eyes in one jar. White with
black eyes in another. The red ones alone, too.

The green of mung in smaller container.
All veiled by glass and stupor.

I take the green of mung from their place
and put a seed into my son's outstretched hands

to feel and to hold. Water is poured over
his cupped palms. Its touch pounds to the inside.

The seed, still at first, moves. Its outer
cover ripples and soon the enclosed one stirs,

bursts out a noise that brings smiles to the two of us.
The eye blinks its darkened center, splits the shell

vertebrate. An arm jerks from the sleeve,
reaches for leverage, finds balance,

spreads open the closure of covering,
steps forward, bids hello and saunters

through the door. My son moves to another jar.
He wants to see more dances of life.

CLOUD COLLECTING

I began in Humboldt Bay, 9 months old, on the hood
of my parents' '47 Pontiac, posing for a photograph,
hands reaching for the white sky, the sheets of clouds
hung over the Pacific on an unseen line. What did I know—
bits of cotton, bread crumbs trailing off to nowhere,
white caps across the wind-washed blue… .
But what did I care, my mind up there, as I ran around
the school yard in my ivory shirt, or along the foothills
of Montecito, gathering the rust-edged, lavender-
infused clouds of dusk? Scarves, pinwheels, blossoms
before the dark, then thunderheads, pillars of chalk, soap flakes,
lint, and even rows of French loaves, scallop shells, mares' tails,
feathered afterthoughts in an old buttermilk sky…angel wings
and fish bones, the palace domes of snow, a nautilus outlining
the blue chambers of air, and one, I think, very like a whale.
And sauntering above the horizon, several seaward in their Latin robes—
cumulus, cirrus, altostratus—the grey-dark nimbus tumbling
down, the dots and dashes of hope we cannot reach—changelings,
reinventing themselves from next to nothing. And far now,
through the Hubble telescope, gas clouds in the deeps cosmos
with their starry buds of light—the loose shape, perhaps, of the soul,
if there is one, if God was an abstract thinker? Come to me,
nevertheless, let me fill my arms with all that I am worth.

COLLECTING

Up hollow, my neighbor chocks
a boneyard of Fords, carcasses he strips
to flesh the one running.

His angular wife
fondles racks of baby spoons,
assembled vertebrae.

Everyone I know is collecting:
calluses, winces, names that tell
who they must and cannot be,

girls' numbers, facial hair, and attitudes,
slogans, speeding tickets, guns,
diagnoses, belly fat, and wives.

Me, I'm dumping the catalogs,
unlabeling the roses,
giving the packrats free run.

Call me a collector of clouds:
the broody one over Wilbur Lake
and its hatchling streamers;

that black one, a sky mountain,
the sun hollering glory behind it
coming home from Moccasin Creek;

this morning's field of cirrus,
furrows softening,
over my seedy meadow.

First I hold still and open,
like a big-mouth bass sculling upstream,
and the cloud slides in,

skittish or easy, either one,
but sweet as skimmed-off cream
or a hand stroking your hair.

Then I let go,
throw to the winds mounts and fixatives,
even the urge to tell.

My neighbor, tooling up the road,
honks at me planted in a ditch, hands lifted,
eyes shining, shining.

A STRING OF BUTTONS AS PRAYER BEADS

I collect buttons because I'm hopeful, I'm hopeful
because I wish, I pray because I'm hopeful and I
wish—I save buttons to use as Protestant prayer beads—I
put them onto thin soft leather strings, buttons are part
of my daily existence, they fall off my shirt cuffs, collars
and pockets, when I need them to hold tight
they spring free, my lapels flap in the cold wind, my pants'
button pops free under a hard sneeze's weight due to my
unexpected and spontaneous effusive overflows, they
represent to me signs how I must be thankful for my joy—I
hold my prayer button string and I touch my shirt cuff button
and thank God for allowing humans to have red wine; I finger
my coat button and ask God to soften commerce
and the corporate-rich's greedy hearts, I thumb my pants button
and ask the Lord to bless my friends, enemies and me
with an energy abundance so that we maintain healthy body weights
to keep our buttons snapped up, my collar button's so small
it hardly moves on the string, I pat it with my index finger and pray
for wisdom passed on to the smallest lives to the wills
of the largest leaders, my pocket button separates a black
hole from eternal stellar light filled space, I pinky point
at it and ask God to continue to bless other people, my family
and me with wisdom to keep our dark spaces divided, so that we
may focus on all or nearly all that makes us good—
when I finish I hang my button string on my closet doorknob
and hope the power of my thoughts and wishes carry my emerald
meditations off quiet as a fresh-lit incense stick's smoke puff.

THE THEORY OF EVERYTHING

It has something to do with invisible string
rippling out across a universal sunset,
wrapping us up like the perfect brown corded package.

Something to do with the vibration of stars—
how they flicker in tune with each other, humming cosmically.
And though I've never seen this reported anywhere

I also believe it has something to do with dogs.
For who else has such capacity to forgive
an entirely other species? Well, yes, God

but I don't mess around with God.
So in my theory, the wet nose of a dog
fits it in the space where our heart has been cut out.

And after dogs, the pure yellow of lemons,
the affection small children hold for Band-Aids, the urge
to touch a stranger's bald head.

It all has a place in the Theory.
Name it and I will hang it on the clothesline.
Name it, I will chop it up for soup.

What's not to believe, anyway, in a theory
that has room enough for all other theories,
even those that say this Theory is shit?

Sure, the vibration of strings we cannot measure.
And yes, the strings are so fine we haven't
found them yet. One might surmise

this is not about strings, but our desire
for strings. You too are welcome
at this Party of Everything.

Come to my house where
we will speak of aqueducts and whiskers,
we will eat brown bread and touch our feet

under the table. You can tell me
we are not connected, that there is nothing
holding us together.

I will tug your ear and peck you softly on the lips.

THE RIDDLE GAME

Hearken the kestrel's call, its cage
a mess of old newspaper, its runny
crap a smear across the headlines. Arrest,
arrest, the blue jay's cackle. Arrest
the hard-strung crawl of the moth.
In a month, it will be dead again.
Never quit the swamp frogs
and copperheads—as when Brother
quit storing scabs in a baby-food jar
hidden between his boxers. Another time,
when he had a hairy left arm, he showed
it off at the grocery store. The canned tuna
watched from the shelves, as did
the checkbook, peeking from our mother's
unlatched purse. When he told me
about the riddle game in the bowling
alley, I hastened to stump him.
I tricked my ball down the slick alley,
but struck none. I offered him my hallowed
hand-me-down brassiere. Here,
where many breasts had been
before. This too, Brother added
to his name. Soon it was the aviary
we were discussing; soon it was
the sphinx. In the summer
we made a replica out of damp sand
at the beach. In one paw, we stuck
a can of beer, in the other fried chicken.
That was the day, and we loved the day.
The riddle that ended with a man walking
on three legs; I'd always imaged the third leg
as a stretched-out erection he teetered around on—
a horny old man, wobbling towards Ithaka.

ROOM

Your body is barely cold and what
is asked of you but to straighten up
the mess you've left your room in?
Maybe it's not your room exactly—
perhaps its Plato's vision of your room—

but it's hardly in perfect form,
what with the stacks of papers sitting squat
as tortoises on your desk, the glossolalia
of unpaid bills waving from a wicker basket,
the coffee-enameled cups glinting their recognition,
this certainly looks like your room.

Electroplated trophies stand sentry on a shelf
half-full of borrowed books or books
you meant to read. A shoe box stuffed with letters
can wait: you've got all night. The desk
drawer trembles at your touch, its inside a mosaic

of loose change, mostly pennies, a foreign coin or two,
and, rolling in the back, a plastic bottle. You take it in
your hands and shake it like a shaman's rattle.
The six pills you never took don't matter, but you squint
at the prescription, long expired, and wonder
what ailed you in November 1990. You recovered, at any rate,

but now you slump into a chair, considering
just what lies ahead. Look, here's a cup of coffee
hardly worse than other cups you've drunk. And there,
beneath the dresser, a crumpled cigarette,
still serviceable. When you stoop for it you spy

the oldest letter that you own, a binding contract
signed by a grey-eyed girl in kindergarten.
Your loopy scrawl beneath hers swore
you'd never marry anyone but her
at peril of a dollar. You want to make good

on your bet—you never were a welsher—
but you don't even try the telephone.
Instead you shut your eyes and sit and wonder
if you wouldn't die for this clutter, this sadness,
this exquisite disarray.

MOTHER CONTEMPLATES THE CREATOR'S REFRIGERATOR

She' so damned
proud
of them—drawings, songs, the things they say
when they don't know she's listening: she's got to tell
someone, pulls out the thick fistful
of photos that she carries everywhere. When they see her coming,
the angels and the saints start humming,
stare heavenward, try to act
busy, but that's a benefit of being boss—you get to talk about your kids whenever
and however long you want. Still, she knows better
than anyone:
when they make a sudden
leap—metallurgy, Relativity,
Impressionism—she's unbearable for days—all smiles. Used to be
she hung their projects up where everyone could look,
but the night's blank
wall got so crowded that she had
to stick most of them in boxes to sort later, leaving behind
the early, simple ones she still sighs to remember.
It's so much easier
to believe
in them, in their love,
when she can look over her shoulder
and see those spattered, corners-curling offerings there.

I'M STARTING A PLASTIC MENAGERIE

behind the computer, beginning with
Devil Duck and the Human-Flesh Colored Javelina.
They are both against the war, and you must talk to them first.

Here lists the only Atlantis for plastic animals, for godless beast and
praying mantis. Sonar incantations irradiate the waterways, now they all
harken back to you, their Chosen One, setting course for the Sea of Ecstacy.

Surfing for extinct quagga on eBay today, the quadratic aquatic
formula for plastic passenger pigeon and California condor to litter the shore,

my 20,000 beleaguered species under the sea, breeding below a Styrofoam ozone
amid the wells of bestial commotion, an azygous zebra zonked out in the bathysphere
with our warped cassette of whale songs for the kazoo.

The dioramas of my reptile mind are speaking in snakes, flashing the amphibian hi-beams,
one day to meet the media beneath my tongue softly succoring some subtle urge to
succumb, teeny amoebas intoning resuscitations.

A flat-earth eternity waiting for sushi boats piled 2 to 3 high to worm their way across
the miso sea tonight—uh huh, that's the tincture of X, another trophy for atrophy
squid-inking another squamous inkling, plus a Galapagos of possibility
hibernating within these Neanderthal plans, when to go awry
means we are to arrive, and all are well and welcome
to the underwater bonfire, and all your
deep-sea manatees come up

for mad, mad air.

WAKING ON ALL SOULS' DAY

The collective noun for a group of crosses?
A crusade? A courage? Don't answer quite yet.
Step, first, into my Room of Crosses.

That crucifix was found at the Santa Fe flea market.
Its font holds an ounce of holy water (not included);
For that I'll need the one who blesses.

A poet who once believed only in conjunctions
Gave me this cross no longer than a haiku.
Now he writes collaborative sonnets in Sanskrit.

Octavio Paz says Mexicans sleep with and celebrate death.
For now I'm content with a day-glow orange cross
Whose skulls wake only on All Souls' Day.

Outside an adobe church on the High Road to Taos
I bought a cross fashioned from two corroded strips
Of tin bound together with rusty wire.

Why is an adverb with limited use.
These crosses, Susan, were never about why.
Why would you even ask?

OFFERING UP THE COLLECTION

The Irish priest had pure white hair,
a black cocker spaniel named Rasputin,
and a glass jar of children's teeth.

An odd collection amassed from years
of tiny gap-smiled visitors bold enough
to cross the street to his brick-faced rectory.

They offered up wadded handkerchiefs,
cradles for bloodied milk-white kernels
that Father praised and plinked into the maw.

In return, he doled out holy trinkets:
small plastic statues of empty-handed Mary
or Jesus pointing to a painted ruby heart.

A cursory sign of the cross over an open mouth
and the child raced back to the playground,
to prove how brave she'd been to go alone.

When confessional boxes murmured dark secrets
and tongues burned down the priest's creed,
his collection hummed like a choir of cherubim.

Rasputin died first, then the priest, in his study.
His jar was flung into the alley, its bit scattered.
All night, the wind sang across drifting snow.

COMPOSURE

Indiana Dunes National Lakeshore, West Beach

I walk the dunes of Lake Michigan and collect
smooth stones
gull feathers   and bird bones

Sometimes
driftwood
if the shape metaphorical
or beach glass
if the color passionate

as if natural debris
could give
a soul
room

as if collection
could deliver
composure

I bend down
on this beach
and break

to pick up pieces of the Earth
in their explanation
for the sanity of death

Bones   Glass   Stones   Feathers

Collecting is taking
back

those thefts we have made
from others

Today I shove into my pockets

returned letters   stones given to me

They expose

my wish
for composure

before the undertow

OFFAL

I have eaten liver in my life:
had the kidneys for it,
and the intestinal fortitude

for brain, tongue, sweetbread of pancreas.
I stomached the brocade of tripe
and still had heart for heart.

I know the symbols of these sacred parts,
The whole canopic jar of them
orbitally displayed upon a rug:

that temple banner beneath the dining table.
There the intestinal mystic knot
lies like a broidered Chinese button.

Then the wheel, the lotus, the umbrella,
the conch, the canopy, the fish.
It's thus I know that flesh feeds flesh

and that they dare not speak of it:
those livers, and those die-ers
because it baffles all their wit.

The shallow stream murmurs in its narrow bed. A wren repeats his signature riff, and redwoods groan in a stiffening breeze. Graffiti on the wall outside says, *I am Valentino Rossi, but not much else.* The world is a gift, a wedding. A woman wipes juice from her child's sticky lips. Someone says, I collect maps. The frozen bolt gives way at last.

Contributors

M. Lee Alexander's poetry has appeared in numerous journals such as *The MacGuffin, The Litchfield Review, Mythic Circle, The Eleventh Muse*, and others. Her work has received many awards, including several first places in the Poetry Society of Virginia Annual Awards, first honorable mention in the Yeats Poetry Contest 2006, and made the shortlist for Bridgport 2009. Her chapbook, *Observatory*, was published by Finishing Line Press in 2007. Alexander teaches creative writing at William and Mary and resides in Williamsburg, VA. She collects children's books, including *Tintin* by Hergé.

Former poet laureate of Milwaukee, **Antler** is the author of *Factory* (City Lights), *Last Words* (Ballantine), *Selected Poems* (Soft Skull), *Exclamation Points Ad Infinitum!, Subterranean Rivulet, A Second Before It Bursts, Open Bible With A Gun On It*, and *Ever-Expanding Wilderness.* Winner of the Walt Whitman Award, a Pushcart Prize, and the Witter Bynner Prize from the American Academy & Institute of Arts & Letters, his poems appear in recent anthologies, including *Poets Against War; An Eye for an Eye Makes the Whole World Blind: Poets on 9/11; Wild Song: Poems from Wilderness; Earth Prayers; Best Gay Poetry of 2008; Poetic Voices Without Borders;* and *Celebrate America in Poetry & Art.*

The Dachau stone resides in his living room on a shrine that includes a fossil trilobite; a baby beaver skull; an arrowhead Allen Ginsberg found as a child and gave to him before he died; a stone from the top of Mt. Snowden that Wordsworth climbed at the end of his poem, "The Prelude"; grave soil from Keats', Shelley's, and Whitman's graves; and a Sequoia cone from the Grizzly Giant.

Gustavo Adolfo Aybar is a graduate of the University of Missouri-Kansas City where he received his MA in Romance Languages & Literature. As a scholar he's presented at the University of Florida and has upcoming publications by ABC-CLIO and Salem Press. He is a Cave Canem fellow, and as a board member with the Latino Writer's Collective, his work can be found in their anthology, *Primera Pagina: Poetry from the Latino Heartland* (Scapegoat Press, 2008). Other publications include: *Harvest of New Millennium*; *Black Magnolias Literary Journal*; *Nine: A Journal of Baseball History & Culture*; *Oranges & Sardines*; and presentmagazine.com where he was a Poet-In-Residence during 2010.

"My poem is simply the sad truth of immigration and the loss of family that occurs when members move away in search of an American or any dream."

Jackie Bartley has published two full-length collections and five chapbooks of poetry. Individual poems have appeared in *Willow Review, The Chaffin Journal, Southern Humanities Review, William and Mary Review,* and many other journals. Having sewed all her life, she has a large collection of fabric scraps. A few years ago, in order to rid herself of some of these scraps, she began quilting. She now has more fabric scraps than she did when she started.

Jeanne Marie Beaumont is the author of three poetry collections, *Burning of the Three Fires* (BOA Editions, 2010), *Curious Conduct* (BOA Editions, 2004), and *Placebo Effects*, which was a National Poetry Series Winner (Norton, 1997). Her work has appeared widely in anthologies and magazines, including *Good Poems for Hard Times, Mondo Barbie, The Year's Best Fantasy and Horror, Poetry Daily, Boston Review, The Nation*, and *World Literature Today*. Her poem, "Afraid So", was made into an award-winning short film, narrated by Garrison Keillor. With Claudia Carlson, she edited *The Poets' Grimm: 20th Century Poems from Grimm Fairy Tales*. Beaumont teaches in the Stonecoast low-residency MFA program and at the Unterberg Poetry Center of the 92nd Street Y. She lives in Manhattan with her husband and cats, along with several tribes of vintage dolls, which she has been photographing since 1992.

Robin Becker, Liberal Arts Research Professor of English at Penn State University, has received fellowships from the Massachusetts Cultural Council, the National Endowment for the Arts, and the Bunting Institute at Harvard University. Her published collections include *Giacometti's Dog, All-American Girl, The Horse Fair,* and *Domain of Perfect Affection,* all in the Pitt Poetry Series. Becker serves as Contributing and Poetry Editor for the *Women's Review of Books* where her column on the contemporary poetry scene, "Field Notes", appears regularly. During the 2010-2011 academic year, Becker served as the Penn State Laureate.

"Years ago, I received, as a gift, *The World of Donald Evans* (Harlan Quist Book, 1980), and I have remained fascinated with Donald Evans and his stamps ever since."

Candace Black teaches at Minnesota State University, Mankato. Her book of poetry, *The Volunteer,* was published by New Rivers Press in 2003, and individual poems have appeared most recently in *Third Coast, RHINO,* and *Colere.* She does not collect blue and white porcelain.

"Except for photos of door knobs, cast iron work, water towers, and graffiti that I take when I travel and then turn into screen savers, I consider myself a passive collector, in that I don't search for things to add to or complete my collections but tend to keep what comes to me: postcards (but only those that have been mailed), rocks or shells I pick up when I travel, wine bottle corks. I recently visited three houses owned by Pablo Neruda—the king of collectors!—and am inspired to be bolder and more whimsical about what I treasure and how I display it."

A graduate of the Iowa Writers' Workshop, **Sean Brendan-Brown** currently resides in Olympia, WA. A medically-retired Marine, he works as a photographer for the Insurance Commissioner's Investigative Division (affectionately called "the yuck unit") and has published with *Notre Dame Review, Wisconsin Review, Southampton Review, Hunger Magazine,* and the University of Iowa Press anthologies, *American Diaspora* and *Like Thunder.* His new chapbook, *The West Is A Golden Paradise,* was released by Litsam Press, Seattle, WA. Sean received a 1997 Fellowship in Poetry and a 2010 Fellowship in Fiction, both from the National Endowment for the Arts.

"My wife and I are fond of antiques, old books and art prints; we haunt the local shops and flea markets for that elusive bargain/treasure and visit garage sales and auctions most weekends. 'Holiday List' is about a week spent at Cannon Beach, OR, one of our favorite places to vacation. It was memorable since nothing seemed to go right, and yet we had so much fun together."

Bill Brown, Karla Scherer Distinguished Service Professor in American Culture, teaches in the departments of English, Visual Arts, and the History of Culture at the University of Chicago. He is a leading expert on object culture, including the practice and art of collecting. His interests in this field range from visual sources, literary texts, and material cultures to the influence objects assert in transforming human beings, individually and collectively. His major theoretical work is in "thing theory", examining the importance of items as they become distinct from the world in which they exist. Dr. Brown's publications include A *Sense of Things: The Object Matter of American Literature; Things,* an award-winning issue of *Critical Inquiry; The Material Unconscious: American Amusement, Stephen Crane, and the Economies of Play;* and *Reading the West: An Anthology of Dime Novels.*

Christopher Buckley's sixteenth book of poetry, *Modern History: Prose Poems 1987-2007,* was published by Tupelo Press in 2008. *Bear Flag Republic: Prose Poems & Poetics from California*, edited with Gary Young, was out from Alcatraz Editions/Greenhouse Review Press in 2008. He was a Guggenheim Fellow in Poetry for 2007-2008, received two National Endowment for the Arts grants, and was awarded the James Dickey Prize for 2008 from *Five Points Magazine.* Buckley, who has edited many anthologies of contemporary poetry and has published two books of creative nonfiction, teaches in the Creative Writing Program at the University of California, Riverside.

Born in San Diego, CA, near the beaches of La Jolla, **W. K. Buckley** received an MA in English and Education at San Diego State University and a PhD from Miami University of Oxford, OH. He teaches at Indiana University NW. His poems have appeared in major journals in America, Canada, and Japan, and he is the author of several chapbooks. Buckley is the editor of *Plath Profiles,* an online, interdisciplinary journal of studies on Sylvia Plath. Buckley collects stones from beaches, from Mount Lemmon in Arizona, and from the mountains around Taos, NM because he believes their ancient shapes and colors hold the energy of time.

Kathryn Stripling Byer lives in the mountains of North Carolina where she has served as the state's Poet Laureate for the past four years. Her six collections of poetry include *Wildwood Flower, Black Shawl, Catching Light,* and most recently, *Coming to Rest,* all from LSU Press. Her work has appeared in journals ranging from *The Atlantic* to *Appalachian Heritage*. Byer has received the Hanes Poetry Award from the Fellowship of Southern Writers, the Southern Independent Booksellers Award for *Catching Light,* the Lamont (now McLaughlin) Award from the Academy of American Poets for *Wildwood Flower,* and fellowships from the National Endowment for the Arts and the North Carolina Arts Council. Hiking in the Smoky Mountains is less grueling for her because of her husband's knowledge of every single plant's name. She collects them in her imagination, along with the names of quilt patterns, ridge-tops, overlooks, and trails.

The author of two books of poetry, *The Broken World* (University of Illinois Press, 1996), a National Poetry Series selection, and *Roman Fever* (Invisible Cities Press, 2001), **Marcus Cafagña's** poems also have appeared in many journals and anthologies, including *DoubleTake, Ploughshares, Poetry, Poets of the New Century, RATTLE,* and *The Southern Review.* Cafagña coordinates the creative writing program at Missouri State University. He collected beer cans as a boy but gave up collecting them before he ever tasted a drop of beer.

Kathleen Cain was an early recipient of a poetry fellowship from the Colorado Council on the Arts. Her poems have appeared in numerous anthologies and magazines, most recently in *Zeus Seduces the Wicked Stepmother in the Saloon of the Gingerbread House, HeartLodge,* and *Pinyon,* with work forthcoming in *Lavanderia: A Mixed Bag of Women, Wash and Word.* She has participated in collaborative *ekphrastic* events with writers and artists, including *Interwoven Illuminations* at RANE Gallery, in Taos, NM in 2008, and *Look Both Ways* in Lincoln, NE in 2009. She has written for *The Bloomsbury Review* since 1982. In addition to collecting family history from time spent living and traveling in Ireland, Cain collects grey-green Irish porcelain.

Kevin Carollo lives in Fargo, ND and teaches world literature and writing at Minnesota State University Moorhead. A regular contributor to *Rain Taxi Review of Books,* he has poems in *Conduit, Court Green, Cranky, Lungfull!,* and elsewhere. He is the winner of *Cream City Review's* 2009 Beau Boudreaux Poetry Prize, has translated two novels from French (*La maestra* by Vénus Khoury-Gata and *The Invention of Renown* by Patrice Nganang), and he rocks with The New Instructions. He collected pop cans and cigar boxes growing up.

Alex Cigale's poems recently appeared in *Colorado, Global City, Green Mountains,* and *North American* reviews, *Drunken Boat, Hanging Loose, McSweeney's, Redactions, Tar River Poetry,* and *32 Poems.* His translations from the Russian can be found in *Crossing Centuries: the New Generation in Russian Poetry, Cimarron Review, Literary Imagination, Modern Poetry in Translation, PEN America, Brooklyn Rail Intranslation,* and *The Manhattan* and *St. Ann's* reviews. Cigale was born in Chernovtsy, Ukraine, has lived in New York City, and is Assistant Professor at the American University of Central Asia in Bishkek, Kyrgyzstan.

"Collecting is our vestigial response to shortage, loss, and the eventuality of extinction, conditioned hoarding in advance of lean times. 'These fragments I have shored against my ruins.' Materials thus preserved, objectifying loss, give things symbolic permanence. So it is with memories. Other, more pleasurable instincts are awakened, currency for our needs of exchange and socialization, the satisfactions of expansiveness, novelty, and variety."

Nicole Cooley grew up in New Orleans. She has published four books of poetry and a novel. Her book of poems, *Breach,* about Hurricane Katrina and its aftermath, appeared with LSU Press in 2010, and *Milk Dress* came out the same year with Alice James Books. She has received the Walt Whitman Award, the Emily Dickinson Award from the Poetry Society of America, and a fellowship from the American Antiquarian Society. She directs the new MFA Program in Creative Writing and Literary Translation at Queens College-CUNY. Cooley is currently working on a new book of poems titled *Artificial Curiosities,* based on her research at small museums across the United States, including a dime museum, a bottle museum, a shoe museum, a clock museum, and a lock museum, among others.

Peter Cooley was born and educated in the Midwest (BA Shimer College, MA University of Chicago, PhD University of Iowa) but has lived half his life in New Orleans where he teaches at Tulane University. He has published eight books of poems, seven of them with Carnegie Mellon, and that press released his most recent, *Divine Margins,* in 2009.

"Although I like to consider myself a 'collector', my wife considers me a 'hoarder'. I have great difficulty letting go of almost anything—from yesterday's newspaper to a letter sent me fifty years ago when I was at camp in Minnesota. The death of everyone in my family—my mother, sister, and father—in the year 2000 sent my collecting habit into high gear. Much as I warn my students about transcribing 'real life', the objects in my poem are those I brought back from Michigan to New Orleans after the three deaths. I have read that the collector (hoarder!) collects in fear of death and that the collecting habit is an attempt to hold back the inevitable. Much as this sounds like pop psychology, it fits my circumstance. By filling my New Orleans life with artifacts from the past, I hoped to create the tomb of an Egyptian pharaoh where immortality could be achieved."

Barbara Daniels' *Rose Fever: Poems* was published by WordTech Communications in 2008. She received two Individual Artist Fellowships from the New Jersey Council on the Arts, was awarded a full fellowship from the Geraldine R. Dodge Foundation to the Vermont Studio Center, and earned an MFA in poetry at Vermont College. Her chapbook, *The Woman Who Tries to Believe,* won the Quentin R. Howard Prize. More than 250 of her poems have appeared in literary journals. Every possible space in the small house she shares with her husband David is filled with books.

A Montana native, **Joshua Doležal** is an erstwhile wilderness ranger and a teacher at Central College in Iowa. His work has most recently appeared in *Fourth Genre, Third Coast, Hudson Review, Gettysburg Review, The Kenyon Review, Hotel America,* and *Brink Magazine.* His poetry has also aired on public radio.

"The more I learn about how memory works, the more I think of it as reassembling experience, sometimes even creating experience. I read about Chinghai Plateau while working as a wilderness ranger in northern Idaho, and the image of the prisoners breaking their backs on road construction in frigid conditions left a deep impression on me. When I began using a pickax again the next time I took my crew out on the trail, I couldn't help but imagine that experience in contrast to what I had read, so that even as I was remembering Chinghai Plateau, I was reassembling that narrative in terms of my own work, and even as I was gathering new experiences and images, they were being shaped by my memory. So memory, to me, is about more than just collecting, and I wonder if in the act of collecting impressions and images about the world around me, perhaps it is I who am being gathered up by a larger narrative."

Wendy Drexler's poems have appeared in *Barrow Street, Brooklyn Review, The Comstock Review, Concho River Review, HeartLodge, The Mid-America Poetry Review, Nimrod* (semi-finalist *Nimrod*/Hardman Pablo Neruda Prize), *Passager, RHINO 2007,* and other journals, and in the anthology, *Blood to Remember: American Poets on the Holocaust*. Her poem, "Earth," was featured on versedaily.com. Drexler's chapbook, *Drive-Ins, Gas Stations, the Bright Motels* (Pudding House, 2007) was nominated for the Pushcart Prize, and her book, *Western Motel,* is forthcoming in April, 2012 (WordTech Communications). By day, she is an editor of language arts materials.

"My 'Adam' persona poem is undoubtedly a projection of my 'collecting' personality. As a child, I was a fanatical collector—matchbooks, buttons, stamps, trading cards, marbles, gemstones. My best friend and I went house-to-house asking neighbors for their unwanted playing cards to add to our trading card collection. Might it have been that attentiveness to objects and their accumulation brought a measure of control to a child whose parents divorced when she was six, providing a way to get her weekend father to buy into her collections, literally and figuratively?"

Denise Duhamel's most recent books are *Ka-Ching!* (University of Pittsburgh Press, 2009), *Two and Two* (Pittsburgh, 2005), *Mille et un Sentiments* (Firewheel, 2005), *Queen for a Day: Selected and New Poems* (Pittsburgh, 2001), The *Star-Spangled Banner* (Southern Illinois University Press, 1999), and *Kinky* (Orchises Press, 1997). A bilingual edition of her poems, *Afortunada de mí* (*Lucky Me*), translated into Spanish by Dagmar Buchholz and David Gonzalez, came out in 2008 with Bartleby Editores (Madrid). Duhamel, who teaches at Florida State University in Miami, collects chapbooks and troll dolls.

Susan J. Erickson is a poet and collage artist who lives in Bellingham, WA. Her poetry has appeared in *Clackamas Literary Review, Raven Chronicles, Switched-on Gutenberg, PoetryMagazine.com, The Lyric,* and various anthologies. Her chapbook, *The Art of Departure,* was published by Egress Studio Press and was recognized as a notable chapbook by newpages.com.

Comic strips from Dubble Bubble gum featuring the twin brothers Dub and Bub were Susan's first collection. Her childhood marble collection included many admired steelies supplied by her mechanic father. Susan began collecting crosses and sun faces when she lived in Tucson, AZ, inspired by the multicultural folk artists of the Southwest.

John Fitzpatrick received Vermont Studio Center poetry residencies, the Hackney Poetry Literary Award, honors in *City Works, Mad Poets Review, Confluence,* and *Taproot Literary Review,* with other poems published in *Mid-America Poetry Review, California Quarterly, Georgetown Review, Cape Rock, Plainsongs, SLAB, Common Ground Review, Oracle,* and others. His doctoral dissertation at New York University treated poet as writer and reader of poetry, with poets Barbara Unger and Michael Burkard participating in his research. Fitzpatrick lives in the Hudson River Valley village of Rhinebeck, NY.

"I collected beans for sprouting, cooking, planting, in small glass jars on the kitchen floor in a secluded country house. When family members stayed, including Schmidt given at birth my mother's maiden name, these jars went spinning everywhere. My poem explores 'Creation' in bean world, in human world, too, for living life with inquiry, joy, fulfillment."

Sharon Foley lives in Whitefish Bay, WI with her husband and children. Though she has come to love the silver waters of Lake Michigan, she still yearns for the white-hot sun of her Nebraska youth. Her writing has most recently appeared in *Plainsongs, Bellowing Ark,* and *White Pelican Review.*

"I have been a collector for as long as I can remember. My children sigh in resignation whenever we happen on estate sales. I spend hours ravaging the tables looking for small items which I later reassemble in shadow boxes. In a similar way, I also collect words for reassembly in my poems. To me, 'The Urn' illustrates the fine line between collecting and obsession, the solace and its danger."

Winner of the 2001 National Poetry Book Award from Salmon Run Press, **CB Follett** has four collections of poetry, the most recent, *And Freddie Was My Darling* (Many Voices Press, 2009). She is publisher/editor of Arctos Press, including the anthology, *GRRRRR, A Collection of Poems About Bears*; the publisher and co-editor of *RUNES, A Review of Poetry,* 2001-2008; and has been nominated for numerous Pushcart Prizes.

"As I am also a collage artist, I am an inveterate collector. It's in the blood. One of my favorite collections is fossilized sand dollars, which wash up on a nearby beach, having broken from an off-shore reef and tumbled onto shore. From quarter size to larger than my palm, they are beautiful and silent witness to a long ago past. As for my poem, 'Word Gathering', one of my earliest mentors was the dedicatee, Ellery Akers, a wonderful poet and teacher. She loves verbs and the pulse they give to poems."

Madelyn Garner has led the educational community as a creative writing instructor, administrator, and editor. Her professional work has been recognized with numerous honors, including the Colorado Governor's Award for Excellence in the Arts and Humanities. She is the recipient of fellowships and prizes for her writing, including the Aspen Writers' Conference Fellowship, the D.H. Lawrence Award from the University of New Mexico, the Jackson Hole Writers Conference Poetry Prize for 2010, and the Robinson Jeffers Tor House Honorable Mention for 2011. Garner's poetry has appeared in literary journals such as *Margie,*

Harpur Palate, Saranac Review, Water-Stone Review, PMS poemmemoirstory, American Journal of Nursing, and the anthology, *Beyond Forgetting, Poetry and Prose about Alzheimer's Disease.*

"My passion for all things beautiful includes Midcentury-Modern-Style furniture and pottery. As executor of noted Hollywood photographer Bradley Braverman's art estate, I design and produce gallery showings of my son's collected works."

Veronica Golos is the author of *Vocabulary of Silence* (Red Hen Press, 2011), an exploration of war and its witnessing-from-afar, and *A Bell Buried Deep,* co-winner of the Nicholas Roerich Poetry Prize (Story Line Press). She has lectured on Teaching Poetry to Children at Columbia University's Teacher's College and Colorado State College. Golos' work has been widely published and anthologized nationally and internationally, including *Meridians, Drunken Boat, Orbus* (London), and *Liqueur 44* (Paris). She has performed at the Nuyorican Café, Lincoln Center, and Cornelia Street Café, in New York City, and at many venues in the Southwest.

"I was intrigued by the inner compulsion of collecting. The need involved in it. It reminded me of a gambler's compulsion, the feeling that 'it' is right around the corner, just past your peripheral vision."

Kimiko Hahn is the author of eight collections of poetry, most recently *Toxic Flora* (W.W. Norton, 2010). A Guggenheim Fellow, she teaches in the MFA Program in Creative Writing and Literary Translation at Queens College, The City University of New York.

"I grew up in a family of not atypical packrats, but aside from the stash of margarine tubs and shopping bags 'to be reused', my artist-parents had amazing art and folk art around the house which they rotated according to season and whim. Crèche, angels, Santas for Christmas; Hindu statues or Italian puppets or Japanese water-droppers for calligraphy–as the spirit moved them. Several years ago, when my husband began a collection of antique poison bottles while writing on a female serial killer, I too began collecting in earnest. In a little shop in Provincetown, we found an Occupied Japan doll in quasi-Chinese garb. I now have nearly a hundred of these figures, all Asian-looking, almost none in kimono. They are more bizarre than 'cute', which is one reason I like them. As far as my poem, I suppose it's an exploration of why we collect. No terrier was harmed in the making of this poem."

Living in Noti, OR, **Quinton Hallett** has three chapbooks, *Quarry, Shiver Quench Slake,* and *Refuge from Flux.* Her work has appeared in *Windfall, hipfish, The Medulla Review, HeartLodge,* and *Tiger's Eye.* She is chair of the Oregon Poetry Association's Eugene-Springfield Chapter, and through OPA, she coordinates poet visits to a rural high school.

"Much of it boils down to marrying something to the void, gathering objects in a circle of high regard. Worry dolls intrigue for their reputation for carrying intangibles...and since I place medicine on most everything in range, I think of collections as holding far more than their physical manifestations."

Michael Hanner was born in Davenport, IA but grew up in Rock Island, IL and Miami, FL. He graduated from the University of Illinois and lived in Chicago until moving to Oregon in 1970. In Eugene, he worked as an architect for 35 years. Hanner is a member of Red Sofa Poets. Hanner's poetry has appeared in *Denali, Tiger's Eye, Margie,* the CD *Poets Demanding Ink,* and several anthologies. He has published a number of chapbooks, including the most recent, *Closing Down the Piccolo Bar,* poems from Italy in 2008, and *Palm Sunday* in 2009.

"The stamp collection of my grandfather sits behind me in an old military chest and a cardboard box. These have been mine since 1949 when he died. For sixty years they have followed me, loyal dogs."

James Harms has published six book of poetry, most recently *After West* (Carnegie Mellon University Press, 2008), *What to Borrow, What To Steal* (Marick Press, 2011), and *Comet Scar* (Carnegie Mellon University Press, 2012). His second collection, *The Joy Addict,* for which he received the PEN/Revson Fellowship, was reprinted in 2009 in the Classic Contemporaries Series. Newer work has appeared or is forthcoming in *Gettysburg Review, Oxford American, West Branch, Poetry International, Quarterly West, Gulf Coast, Drunken Boat, Barrelhouse,* and others. A recipient of a National Endowment for the Arts Fellowship and three Pushcart Prizes, he is Professor of English at West Virginia University where he was the founding director of the MFA Program in Creative Writing. He also directs the low-residency MFA Program in Poetry at New England College.

"It seems to me that it's the child within us who does most of the collecting, so now that I have four children, I collect vicariously through them, as my poem suggests."

A native of eastern Washington State, **Mark D. Hart** lives in western Massachusetts where he is a psychotherapist, the guiding teacher for a Buddhist community, and an adjunct religious advisor at Amherst College. His poetry has appeared or is forthcoming in *RATTLE, Poetry East, The Midwest Quarterly, The Spoon River Poetry Review,* and *Tar River Poetry.* He does not collect rejection slips; those are recycled immediately. He likes to collect the sap of life and boil it down into poetry.

Marie Henry is a San Francisco-born poet and short fiction writer now living in San Rafael, CA. Her work has appeared in numerous literary journals, including *RUNES, Barnabe Mountain Review, Exquisite Corpse,* and in such anthologies as *Full Court: A Literary Anthology of Basketball* and *Nixon Under the Bodhi Tree and Other Works of Buddhist Fiction.* Henry's collections include string (harps and guitars) and frequent swimmer miles (mostly in laps, but also ranging from traversing the Red Sea to swimming across the Golden Gate). She also has a bad habit of collecting years of not being able to function...which, after three long decades, just got traced back to the bite of a tick.

Mary Crockett Hill is the author of *A Theory of Everything* (winner of the Autumn House Poetry Prize) and *If You Return Home with Food* (winner of the Bluestem Poetry Award). She lives in Virginia. For almost a decade, Crockett

Hill worked as a history museum director where she daily met people who collected everything from curling irons to chalkware string dispensers. She has attempted to avoid collecting things in her own home; however, friends have told her that she does have a "book problem". Her poem, "A Theory of Everything", is about the unlikely attempt to collect all ideas into a single theory.

Jane Hirshfield is the author of the newly published *Come, Thief* (Knopf, 2011), six earlier award-winning collections of poetry, including *After* (HarperCollins, 2006), and a now-classic book of essays, *Nine Gates: Entering the Mind of Poetry* (HarperCollins, 1997). She also has collected and co-translated the work of women poets of the past in three much-reprinted anthologies. Her awards include major fellowships from the Guggenheim and Rockefeller foundations, the National Endowment for the Arts, and the Academy of American Poets. Her work has appeared in *The New Yorker, The Atlantic, The Nation, The New Republic,* and many literary magazines, as well as six editions of *The Best American Poetry* and several *Pushcart Prize* anthologies.

Featured on *Poetry Daily, Verse Daily, The Writer's Almanac,* and *The Best of the Net,* **Paul Hostovsky's** work has won a Pushcart Prize, the Muriel Craft Bailey Award from *The Comstock Review,* and chapbook contests from Grayson Books, Riverstone Press, and the Frank Cat Press. His first full-length collection, *Bending the Notes,* is available from Main Street Rag, and his new book of poems, *A Little in Love a Lot,* was published in 2011 by Main Street Rag.

Christina Hutchins has worked as a biochemist and a Congregational (UCC) minister and currently teaches at Pacific School of Religion, Berkeley. Recent poems appear in *Antioch Review, Beloit Poetry Journal, Denver Quarterly, The Missouri Review, The New Republic, Prairie Schooner, The Southern Review,* and *Women's Review of Books.* In addition to two chapbooks, *Collecting Light* (Acacia Books, 1999) and *Radiantly We Inhabit the Air* (Seven Kitchens Press, Becker Prize, 2011), her poetry collection, *The Stranger Dissolves,* was published by Sixteen Rivers Press in 2011. A second book, *World Without,* has been a finalist for Tupelo's Dorset Prize and the National Poetry Series. She has won *The Missouri Review* Editors' Prize, the Villa Montalvo Poetry Prize, received two Barbara Deming Awards, and serves as Poet Laureate of Albany, CA. Hutchins collects *words,* plain old rocks from beloved places (the best paperweights), long light, human love, and the felt textures of fences, sculptures, leaves, napes, grass, wrought iron.

Born and raised in Denver, CO, **Joseph Hutchison** graduated from the University of Northern Colorado in 1972 and received an MFA from the University of British Columbia in 1974. He has published 12 collections of poems, including *The Rain at Midnight, Bed of Coals* (winner of the 1994 Colorado Poetry Award), *House of Mirrors, The Undersides of Leaves,* and the 1982 Colorado Governor's Award volume, *Shadow-Light.* His poetry, fiction, and essays have appeared in over 100 journals and several anthologies. Hutchison lives with his wife, Melody Madonna, in the mountains southwest of Denver and makes his living as a writer and educator.

"'At the Arts Fundraiser' is faithful to my memory of a real event. Beyond that fact, it's important to note that the speaker protests internally against being 'collected' but doesn't attempt to escape the collection. As usual, artists often grant themselves the privilege of having things both ways."

Jayne Fenton Keane is the author of three poetry books, three poetry radio plays, two poetry web installations, and is a tutor of Creative and Digital Writing subjects at Griffith University in Australia. She holds a PhD in spatial poetics and is the recipient of several major national awards, scholarships, and fellowships, including a Research Fellowship at the Ornithology and Bio-Acoustics Laboratories at Cornell University in 2005. Residencies at the National Science and Technology Museum in Taiwan, Rimbun Dahan Artists' Studio (Malaysia), Atlantic Centre for the Arts, and CGH Earth have given her practice and scholarship a global and interdisciplinary focus.

"I am an avid collector of shiny, heart-shaped rocks; also the not so shiny; even the poor, dull stone hidden under dirt."

Susan Kenyon has written poetry all her life. Her book, *Petal on the Tongue,* was published by The Edwin Mellen Press. She has a second book looking for a home. She was West Coast Director for the Great Books Foundation Discussion Program.

"To understand and fully experience the foundation of life, I farmed in Oregon for ten years: sheep, goats, chickens, besides the garden. It made me a non-rigid vegetarian. I would hate to see lambs disappear from the planet; however, only the ewe half of those that are born in the Spring could stay with the flock.

"I was born and grew up in China where my father was director of the English paper, *The North China Daily News & Herald, Ltd.* He enjoyed the fact I'd try anything once. The poem, 'Offal', is one of the results. The temple rug now hangs in my granddaughter's house."

Associate Professor of English at Purdue, **Christian Knoeller** has published poetry in literary journals regularly for several decades, with recent work appearing in the *Evansville Review, Hawai'i Pacific Review, Iron Horse, South Dakota Review,* and *Westview.* His first collection, *Completing the Circle,* was awarded the Millennium Prize by Buttonwod Press, and another, *Learning to Tell Time,* is in progress. He has taught writing, literature, and English Education at the college level for the past twenty years, including creative writing courses as well as a variety of graduate seminars, most recently Writing in Middle and Secondary School. Knoeller was awarded the Jill Barnum Midwestern Heritage Prize in 2007 and recently elected President of the Society for the Study of Midwestern Literature.

William Kupinse is Associate Professor of English at the University of Puget Sound where he teaches British modernism, ecocriticism, and creative writing. His poems have appeared in *Cascade, Cimarron Review, The Fourth River,* and elsewhere, as well as in his book, *Fallow* (2009), and the anthology, *Many Trails to the Summit: Poems by Forty-Two Pacific Northwest Poets* (2010). His campus office currently features a collection that includes seven dirty coffee cups, one in-process poetry manuscript, and every student paper that hasn't been picked up since 2003.

J. Keiko Lane is a fourth generation Japanese American poet, essayist, professor, and psychotherapist. A Los Angeles native, she is the daughter of a jazz musician and a painter, and she now lives in the Bay Area with her partner and family. A collector of books from an early age, she started writing, collecting, and archiving letters and stories in her AIDS activist community in the 1990s, trying to preserve stories, memories, and connections in the midst of epic loss. She is a past winner of the Barbara Mandigo Kelly Peace Poetry Award of the Nuclear Age Peace Foundation. Her poetry and essays have appeared in numerous journals and anthologies, including *Americas Review, The Harrington Lesbian Fiction Quarterly, The Poetry of Peace,* and *Sex and Single Girls.*

Wayne Lee's poems have appeared in *New Millennium, The Ledge, California Quarterly, New England Anthology of Poets, Writer's Digest, Steam Ticket, Sage Trail, Poemeleon, Poetry Motel, Poets Against War, The Floating Bridge Anthology,* and other journals and anthologies. His awards include the Emily Dickinson Award in Poetry, the William Stafford Award in Poetry, the Robert Penn Warren Award, the Charles Proctor Humor Award, *Writer's Digest* Writing Awards, and the *Santa Fe Reporter's* War and Peace Poetry Contest. His chapbooks include *Doggerel & Caterwauls: Poems Inspired by Cats and Dogs* (Red Mountain Press, 2011), and (with his wife, Alice Morse Lee) *Twenty Poems from the Blue House* (Whistle Lake Press, 1998).

Wayne Lee loves found objects, including beach glass. He has spent countless blissful hours combing for white, green, brown. and blue fragments, polished smooth by Mother Nature. From them, he has made stained (beach) glass windows, mobiles, jewelry, and more.

An award-winning poet, **Laura LeHew's** work appears in a myriad of national and international journals and anthologies, including *Eating Her Wedding Dress: A Collection of Clothing Poems* from Ragged Sky Press, *HeartLodge, Her Mark Calendar 2007* and *2009, PMS,* and The Syracuse Cultural Workers' *Women Artists Datebook 2010.* Her chapbook, *Beauty,* was recently released by *Tiger's Eye* Press. She received her MFA in writing from the California College of the Arts, a writing residency from Soapstone, and interned for *CALYX Journal.* Laura is busy spinning up a new press, Uttered Chaos.

LeHew does keep all the letters, cards, emails that are sent to her. Photos are neatly stored in boxes organized by year. The stilettos, leather bra and teddys have given way to orthotics, support, and comfort. She still has the key. (And the cuffs.)

Rebecca Lehmann has published poems in *Tin House, Indiana Review, Denver Quarterly, Columbia Poetry Review, RATTLE,* and *Makeout Creek,* among other journals. Her first book, *Between the Crackups,* won the Salt Crashaw Prize and is forthcoming from Salt Publishing. She has been awarded a Maytag Fellowship from the Iowa Writers' Workshop, from which she holds an MFA, and an artist residency at the Millay Colony for the Arts. Lehmann has just completed a PhD in English at Florida State University and is Visiting Assistant Professor of English at Viterbo University in La Crosse, WI.

"When writing 'The Riddle Game', I thought a lot about the collected images of my childhood. I don't actually have a brother my age, but I always wanted one when I was a child, so in this poem I imagined what it would have been like to have one. In the poem, I've also concentrated on riddle games, which were a custom in many ancient cultures, and represent the act of collecting language."

Lyn Lifshin's newest book is entitled, *All the Poets Who Have Touched Me, Living and Dead: All True, Especially the Lies,* (World Parade Books, 2010). Other recent books include *The Licorice Daughter, Mirrors, Desire, 92 Rapple Drive, Lost in the Fog, Persephone, Nutley Pond, Barbaro: Beyond Brokenness,* and *Light at the End.* Her last two Black Sparrow books, *Cold Comfort* and *Before It's Light,* won *The Paterson Literary Review* Award. She has published over 120 books, edited four anthologies, and is the subject of a documentary film, *Lyn Lifshin: Not Made of Glass.*

"I don't seem to really collect much. Books maybe, horse books when I was writing about Ruffian and Barbaro...poetry books always and maybe not such a great thing to collect: too much velvet, too many clothes."

Ellaraine Lockie has published seven chapbook collections and serves as Poetry Editor for the lifestyles magazine, *Lilipoh.* She has received eleven Pushcart Prize nominations, the Lois Beebe Hayna Award from *The Eleventh Muse,* the One Page Poem Prize from the Missouri Writers' Guild, the Writecorner Press Poetry Award, the Skysaje Poetry Prize, the Dean Wagner Poetry Prize, and the Elizabeth R. Curry Prize from *SLAB.* Recently released are *Mod Gods and Luggage Straps,* a poetry/art broadside from BrickBat, and two chapbooks, *Stroking David's Leg,* from FootHills Publishing, and *Love in the Time of Electrons,* from Pudding House Press.

Lockie inherited the collective instinct and, as a small child, began her collection of miniature perfume bottles. Her collections grew with her years, and she now surrounds herself with rabbits in all forms (including live ones), antique candy molds, buttons, silver charms, pop-up books, and handmade papers.

Rachel Loden is the author of *Dick of the Dead* (Ahsahta Press, 2009), which was shortlisted for both the PEN Center USA Literary Award for Poetry and the California Book Award. She is also the author of *Hotel Imperium* (University of Georgia Press), which won the Contemporary Poetry Series Competition. Honors include two appearances in the *Best American Poetry* series, a Pushcart Prize, a fellowship in Poetry from the California Arts Council, and a grant from the Fund for Poetry.

"In my teens, when I read promiscuously around the clock, I actually did have to think for a moment before putting *Our Lady of the Flowers,* say, on top of *The Complete Poems of Emily Dickinson.* The books were so alive that

I wondered whether they might bruise. Several of the volumes in my poem, 'A Lending Library,' are on my shelves; others are completely invented. A few take an occasional detail from the catalogs of bibliophiles, which I like to peruse as almost a sort of pornography."

Cheryl Loetscher writes from Colorado. Her poems have appeared widely, and a number have won prizes and distinctions in literary contests across the United States. She was awarded the 2008 Douglas Freels Poetry Prize by the FCCJ Writer's Festival, and her first collection of poems, *Unclaimed Baggage*, published by Finishing Line Press in 2007, was awarded the 2008 Jean Pedrick Chapbook Award by the New England Poetry Club. She is not, by nature, a collector of anything tangible that requires dusting.

Christina Lovin is the author of *What We Burned for Warmth* and *Little Fires.* Her writing is widely published in literary journals and anthologies. The Southern Women Writers' Conference awarded Lovin the 2007 Emerging Poet Award, and she received the 2009 Ethnographic Poetry Competition Award for "Myth Information" from the Society for Humanistic Anthropology. Lovin has served as Writer-in-Residence at Devil's Tower National Monument, the H. J. Andrews Experimental Forest in Central Oregon, and as the inaugural Writer-in-Residence at Connemara, Flat Rock, NC, home of the late poet, Carl Sandburg. Her work has been generously supported on several occasions with grants from the Elizabeth George Foundation, the Kentucky Foundation for Women, and the Kentucky Arts Council, including the 2007 Al Smith Fellowship. Lovin makes her home in central Kentucky where she collects wool, dust, rejection letters, and unwanted dogs from the Humane Society.

Alexander Lumans graduated from the MFA Fiction Program at Southern Illinois University Carbondale. His poems have been published or are forthcoming in *Sycamore Review, South Carolina Review, The Collagist,* and *Strange Horizons,* among others. His poetry won first, second, and third places in the 2007 Roxanna Rivera Memorial Poetry Contest, and he won third place in the 2010 Wabash Prize for Poetry. His fiction has been published in *Clarkesworld,* is forthcoming in *Greensboro Review* and *Southern Indiana Review,* and the anthologies, *Surreal South 2009* and *The Versus Anthology.* He now teaches and lives in Boulder, CO.

"When I was a kid, the Valentine Armadillo snuck into my house every Valentine's Day early in the morning before my sister and I got up for school. He left valentine cards all over the house, and according to my parents, who somehow knew his scheme, we could only open our gift baskets from the Armadillo after we had found all of his cards (which never happened). I never really questioned this secret, annual visit to our house until I later discovered that he didn't visit any of my friends' houses. But that only deepened my belief. Of course he only came to one house. He was just an armadillo."

Marie-Elizabeth Mali received an MFA in poetry from Sarah Lawrence College. She is the author of *Steady, My Gaze* (Tebot Bach, 2011), and her work has appeared in *Calyx, Lumina, Tiferet,* and *MiPOesias,* among others. She collects many orange-colored things and images of dragonflies and reef creatures.

Marjorie Manwaring lives in Seattle, WA where she is a freelance writer and co-editor for the online poetry and art journal, the *DMQ Review.* Her work has been published in *Crab Orchard Review, Floating Bridge Review, 5 AM,* and other journals, and her first full-length collection is forthcoming from Mayapple Press in 2013. She has been awarded writing residencies through the Whiteley Center at Friday Harbor on San Juan Island and Artsmith on Orcas Island. Given that her tiny house is stuffed to the rafters with books and mementos, she has taken to collecting small things—charms, poems, and other miniatures.

The 2009 Everglades National Park Artist-in Residence, **Karla Linn Merrifield** has had poetry appear in publications such as *Calyx, Earth's Daughters, Poetica, The Kerf, Negative Capability,* and *Paper Street,* and in several anthologies. In 2006, she edited *The Dire Elegies: 59 Poets on Endangered Species of North America* (FootHills Publishing). In 2007, FootHills issued *Godwit: Poems of Canada* (Andrew Eiseman Writers Award for Poetry). Her new chapbook, *The Urn,* is published by Finishing Line Press. Forthcoming from Finishing Line is *The Ice Decides* and from Salmon Poetry her full-length collection, *Athabaskan Fractal and Other Poems of the Far North.* Merrifield collects places (e.g. Antarctica, the Galapagos, 11 European countries, all 50 U.S. states, and all the Canadian provinces and territories).

John O'Dell's poetry has appeared in The *Potomac Review, The Birmingham Poetry Review, The George Mason Review, The Atlanta Review,* and others. Further work appears in several anthologies, including *Free State: A Harvest of Maryland Poets* and *Hungry As We Are.* O'Dell was a 1997 Individual Artist Award recipient from the Maryland State Arts Council. He is the author of a collection of poems, *Painting at Night* (Little Cove Press, 1994).

"As a child I was always fascinated by the arrowheads and petrified wood my father collected on our farm in Illinois. I am moved by his urge to hold onto the tangible past on a land he loved."

Jessy Randall's collection of poems, *A Day in Boyland* (Ghost Road Press, 2007), was a finalist for the Colorado Book Award. Her young adult novel, *The Wandora Unit,* was published in 2009. In first grade she collected popsicle sticks and plastic bread tags. Now she is the Curator of Special Collections at Colorado College and collects regional menus, tourist brochures, bumper stickers, zines, and other ephemera. She learned of the rarity of the blue mad boy from her friends Amy Shuffelton and Noah Sobe, who collect vintage Fisher Price Little People.

A noted poet and translator, **Carlos Reyes'** latest book of poetry is *At the Edge of the Western Wave* (2004). *The Book of Shadows: New and Selected Poems* is due out next year from Lost Horse Press. *A Suitcase Full of Crows* (1995) was a winner of the Bluestem Award. His most recent book of translations is Ignacio Ruiz Pérez's *La señal del cuervo (The Sign of the Crow).* Reyes was the recipient of The Fortner Award from St. Andrews College, and he has been an Oregon Arts Commission Fellow, a Yaddo Fellow, a Fundación Valparaíso Fellow (Spain), a Heinrich Boll Fellow (Ireland), and most recently was poet-in-residence at the Joshua Tree National Park.

"'Estate' grew out of thinking about the personal effects of my goddaughter/stepdaughter sent back from Brazil when she drowned there in 2001, and estate and yard sales."

Jonathan Rice's poems have been published in *AGNI Online, Colorado Review, Mississippi Review, Sycamore Review,* and *Witness,* among others, and are forthcoming in *Best New Poets 2010, A Face to Meet the Faces: An Anthology of Contemporary Persona Poetry,* and *The Southern Poetry Anthology, Volume V: Georgia.* His poetry was selected for the 2010 Indiana Review Poetry Prize, the 2010 Richard Peterson Poetry Prize from *Crab Orchard Review,* the 2008 Gulf Coast Poetry Prize, the 2008 Milton-Kessler Memorial Prize from *Harpur Palate,* the 2008 Yellowwood Poetry Prize from *Yalobusha Review,* and the 2006 AWP Intro to Journals Awards. He received an MFA from Virginia Commonwealth University and is currently a PhD candidate at Western Michigan University.

Rice collects rocks—and not even valuable ones, like garnets or amethyst, jasper or agate, but lots of mica, flint chips almost shaped like arrowheads, sandstone, shale, granite, and maybe gypsum—while his wife collects sharks' teeth that are actually sharks' teeth, and not just disappointing slivers of black plastic from shredded (probably by real sharks) microwave meal trays, which wash up in the wake of passing cargo ships.

Pattiann Rogers has published ten books of poetry, a book-length essay, *The Dream of the Marsh Wren,* and *A Covenant of Seasons,* in collaboration with the artist, Joellen Duesberry. Her most recent book of poetry is *Wayfare* (Penguin, 2008), and her book, *The Grand Array, Writings on Nature, Science, and Spirit,* was published by Trinity University Press (2010). Rogers is the recipient of two National Endowment for the Arts grants; a Guggenheim Fellowship; a Literary Award in Poetry from the Lannan Foundation; and five Pushcart Prizes, among other awards. Her papers are archived in the Sowell Collection at Texas Tech University. Rogers has taught as a visiting writer at various universities, including the Universities of Texas, Arkansas, and Montana, and Washington University. Rogers has two sons and three grandsons and lives with her husband in Colorado.

"My poem, 'The Composer, the Bone Yard', is a fantasy in which I question what a scientist is actually composing as he collects and assembles the bones of ancient humans and extinct creatures, how that composition might be creating and changing him."

Marjorie Saiser's most recent books are *Rooms* (Pudding House Publications, 2010) and *Beside You at the Stoplight* (The Backwaters Press, 2010), winner of the Little Blue Stem Award. Other publications include *Bones Of A Very Fine Hand* (1999) and *Lost in Seward County* (2001), both from The Backwaters Press, and a chapbook, *Moving On,* from Lone Willow Press. Her work has been published in *The Prairie Schooner, The Georgia Review, Crazy Horse, Smartish Pace, Crab Orchard Review,* and *Cream City Review.* Saiser was named Distinguished Artist for poetry by the Nebraska Arts Council.

"Marjorie Saiser, more's the pity, collects bumps and bruises. She's learning wisdom from close observation of her children."

Penelope Scambly Schott has published a novel, four chapbooks, and six books of poetry. Her most recent works are *May the Generations Die in the Right Order* and a verse biography, *A is for Anne: Mistress Hutchinson Disturbs the Commonwealth,* winner of the Oregon Book Award in Poetry, She has enjoyed fellowships at the Fine Arts Work Center in Provincetown, MA; The Vermont Studio Center in Johnson, VT; and The Wurlitzer Foundation in Taos, NM. At home, she has cooked more than 15,000 dinners, graded more papers than that, spoiled her husband and her dog, taught her grandson things he shouldn't know, and hiked extensively in the Columbia Gorge.

Nancy Scott is the current managing editor of *U.S.1 Worksheets,* the journal of the U.S.1 Poets' Cooperative in New Jersey. She is the author of two books of poetry, *Down to the Quick* (2007) and *One Stands Guard, One Sleeps* (2009), both published by Plain View Press, and two chapbooks, *A Siege of Raptors* (Finishing Line Press, 2010) and *Detours & Diversions* (Main Street Rag, 2011). Nancy began writing poetry in the mid-90s as a way of recording the many stories she'd heard in her decades of advocacy and casework on behalf of abused children, homeless families, and those with AIDS and mental illness.

"I wanted an authentic war rug from the Soviet occupation of Afghanistan and spent several years searching. I finally found one in a shop in Annapolis, MD, owned by an Afghan woman who sent all the proceeds to a women's collective in Afghanistan. I bought many tribal and prayer rugs from her, not only to support her mission but because I thought the rugs were works of art. On eBay, I found a rug seller from New Hampshire, who had access to Afghan rugs. He, too, was sending profits back to Afghanistan to support the building of schools for girls. I share my home with these beautiful rugs."

Peter Schwartz's words have been featured in *PANK, Wigleaf, Opium,* and *The Columbia Review.* He's also an artist, comedian, and dedicated kayaker.

Paula Sergi is the author of *Family Business,* a chapbook of original poems, and the forthcoming chapbook titled *Black Forest Love Songs.* She is the co-editor of three anthologies: *Boomer Girls: Poems by Women from the Baby Boom Generation, Meditations on Hope,* and *A Call to Nursing.* The Wisconsin Academy of Sciences, Arts and Letters, along with the Hessen Literary Society, selected her as the 2005 cultural ambassador to Germany, which included a three-month residency in Wiesbaden. A Wisconsin Arts Board Artist Fellowship recipient, her poetry is widely published, including such journals as *RATTLE, The Bellevue Literary Review, Primavera, Crab Orchard Review,* and *Spoon River Poetry Review.* Her poem, "Gardener", is a meditation on her fascination with and desire for green glassware.

John Oliver Simon has published over 400 translations of contemporary Latin American poets and was awarded a National Endowment for the Arts Literature Fellowship in Translation in 2001. He is Artistic Director of Poetry Inside Out, a program of the Center for the Art of Translation that teaches middle-school students to translate great poetry from Spanish to English. One of his poems is set in bronze in the sidewalk in the Addison Street Poetry Walk in Berkeley, CA. He doesn't collect stuff, particularly.

"'Isla Negra' was written at the house, now a museum, that world-famous poet Pablo Neruda constructed on the rocky coast of Chile and stuffed with ships' figureheads, ships in bottles, butterflies in jars, a life-size wooden horse, and all the miscellany of a life spent collecting things and poems."

Julia Meylor Simpson lives in East Providence, RI and works in corporate communications. She has a BA in journalism from Iowa State University and an MA in English from Rhode Island College. Her poetry has appeared in a number of national and regional journals, including *English Journal, Connecticut River Review, Sojourn, Alligator Juniper,* and *Blue Earth Review.*

Simpson wrote the poem, "Offering Up the Collection", after happening upon a number of wadded-up tissues that held her two daughters' long-gone baby teeth in an old jewelry box. Memories of the peculiar collection of a kind-hearted parish priest came flooding back.

Nancy Simpson, author of *Night Student* and *Across Water* (State Street Press), lives on a mountain in North Carolina. A new and selected collection of her work, *Living Above The Frost Line: New and Selected Poems,* was published in 2010 by Carolina Wren Press. Simpson's poetry has appeared in *The Georgia Review, Southern Poetry Review, Prairie Schooner,* and other literary magazines. Seven of Simpson's poems were featured in a textbook, *Southern Appalachian Poetry* (McFarland Press, 2008), and her poem, "Carolina Bluebirds", was included in *The Poets Guide To The Birds,* edited by Judith Kitchen and Ted Kooser (Anhinga Press, 2009). Simpson earned an MFA from Warren Wilson College and is Resident Writer at John C. Campbell Folk School. Her six-inch corn shuck dolls, made by Appalachian women, remain her favorite collection.

Su Smallen is the author of two books, *Buddha, Proof* and *Weight of Light,* which was nominated for the Pushcart Press Editor's Book Award. Her poems and essays have appeared in *Bellingham Review, The Normal School, Smartish Pace, Three Candles, Water~Stone Review,* and several anthologies. Her many honors include the Jane Kenyon Poetry Prize, judged by Elizabeth Alexander, and grants from the Southeastern Minnesota Arts Council. She teaches in Hamline University's MFA program.

"'A Quieter Art' is inspired by Joseph Cornell's boxes and by my grandfather who, like Cornell, made toys out of things he saved and salvaged. In his basement workroom and in the shed were jars and cans of small pieces of wood, bits of wire, curtain rings, hooks, springs, rubber tips, mysterious metal parts. And a small box of flea collars for the stray cats he fed from a broken-handled skillet."

Mark Smith-Soto is professor of Spanish and editor of *International Poetry Review* at the University of North Carolina at Greensboro. Winner of a 2005 National Endowment for the Arts fellowship in creative writing, he has two full-length poetry collections to date, *Our Lives Are Rivers* (University Press of Florida, 2003) and *Any Second Now* (Main Street Rag, 2006). Three of his chapbooks have been published as winners of literary competitions, and his poetry has appeared in *Antioch Review, Kenyon Review, Literary Review, Nimrod, The Sun,* and numerous other publications. His most recent book is *Fever Season: Selected Poetry of Ana Istarú*, a work of translation published in 2010 by Unicorn Press.

"The basis for 'From the Back of the Closet' was a dusty, small wood box inlaid with bits of mother-of-pearl which I found when sorting out my mother's belongings after her death some years ago. It intrigued me somehow, there was something tantalizingly elusive about its simple contents that I felt compelled to wonder about in a poem...I removed any specific reference to the owner of the box because what really interested me was how people we love and think we know can still remain mysterious to us in unexpected ways."

David Spiering has two university degrees from the University of Wisconsin system. His poetry has appeared in *Poetry East, Mudfish, The Chiron Review,* and *The West Wind Review*, among others, and he has had fiction published as well. Spiering's chapbooks are *Night Driving* (1998), *Dinosaur Catfish* (2002), and *Crooked Litanies* (2005). Sol Books brought out his first full-length collection, *My Father's Gloves,* in 2010.

"I'm always searching for prompts. They take me out of the realm of self-conscious navel-gazing—from playing ring around the belly button. They help me dig into the unknown space where I find unique takes on what I know and feel."

Joseph Stanton's books of poems are *Imaginary Museum: Poems on Art* (a book-length "gallery" of his art-inspired poems); *A Field Guide to the Wildlife of Suburban O'ahu: Poems; Cardinal Points: Poems on St. Louis Cardinals Baseball;* and *What the Kite Thinks: A Linked Poem.* His poems have appeared in such journals as *Poetry, Harvard Review, Poetry East, The Cortland Review, Endicott Studio, Ekphrasis,* and *New York Quarterly.* As an art historian, he has published essays on Edward Hopper, Winslow Homer, Maurice Sendak, and many other artists. His other books include *The Important Books: Children's Picture Books as Art and Literature; A Hawai'i Anthology; Stan Musial: A Biography;* and the forthcoming, *Looking for Edward Gorey.* He is a professor of Art History and American Studies at the University of Hawai'i at Mānoa.

Carol Steinhagen has retired from Marietta College, where she was a professor of English, to take up life as a poet. Her most recently published work can be read in *Future Cycle, Imagination & Place,* and *Rockhurst Review.* Though unsalaried and recession-poor, Steinhagen continues to support her collecting habit, seeking not only botanical prints but a variety of antiques, including bottles, photographs and kitchenware. In a world of uncertainties, poetry and old things keep her attached to the certainties of the past.

Fiona Sze-Lorrain writes and translates in English, French, and Chinese. Her book of poetry, *Water the Moon* (Marick Press, 2010), is an Honorable Mention for the 2011 Eric Hoffer Book Award. A co-editor at Cerise Press, Sze-Lorrain lives in France and is a *zheng* concertist. She enjoys collecting items that contain strong interior life, with historical and personal narratives yet to be revealed.

Australian-born **Katrin Talbot's** collection, *St. Cecilia's Daze,* was recently published by Parallel Press, and her collection, *Freeze-Dried Love,* is forthcoming from Finishing Line Press. Her work has appeared in *The New Plains Review, Fresh Ink, Free Verse, Ginosko, If, Zoland,* and *Manorborn* poetry journals, and in numerous anthologies, such as *Eating Her Wedding Dress: A Collection of Clothing Poems* (Ragged Sky Press). Talbot was a finalist for the 2009 Yellowwood Poetry Prize, the 2009 Artsmith Literary Contest, and *Phoebe Journal's* 2009 Greg Grummer Prize. Her photo-essay book of Schubert's *Winterreise* was published by the University of Wisconsin Press and won an American Library Association Best of the Best of the University Presses Award. She also collects smiles.

Diane Thiel is the author of ten books, including *Echolocations* (Nicholas Roerich Prize*), Resistance Fantasies,* and *The White Horse: A Colombian Journey.* Thiel's translation of Alexis Stamatis's *American Fugue* (National Endowment for the Arts International Literature/Translation Award) appeared in 2008. Thiel's work appears in *Poetry, The Sewanee Review, Best American Poetry 1999,* is reprinted in over fifty major anthologies, and is translated widely. A recipient of many awards, including the Robert Frost and Robinson Jeffers Awards, and a Fulbright Scholar, she is Professor at the University of New Mexico.

"I collect things brought in by the sea (as in the poem included) or the desert wind, or by my children—beach glass, driftwood, pumice, natural objects from around the world. On New Mexico hikes, or on travels, I find my young children's pockets filled with treasures; they have to choose from the thirty rocks they want to take along."

Susan Terris' books include *The Homelessness of Self, Contrariwise*, and *Fire Is Favorable to the Dreamer.* Her work has appeared in many journals, including *The Southern Review, The Journal,* and *Ploughshares.* A poem of hers appeared in *Pushcart Prize XXXI.* She is the editor of *Spillway Magazine* and poetry editor of *In Posse Review* and of *Pedestal.*

"Besides collecting words, I also collect bells, small baskets, and trips down wild rivers."

David Trinidad's books of poetry include *Plasticville* (2000), *The Late Show* (2007), and *Dear Prudence: New and Selected Poems* (2011), all published by Turtle Point Press. He teaches poetry at Columbia College Chicago, where he co-edits the journal *Court Green.*

"'Fluff' was written in the mid-nineties for the Canadian poet Lynn Crosbie, who told me that as a child she'd coveted her friend's Fluff doll. I was actively collecting vintage Barbie dolls at the time, so it was easy to obtain a Fluff for her. As I say in the poem, they were not highly valued in the collecting world. I wrapped the doll in the poem and sent it to Crosbie. She wrote that the gift moved her to tears. I just checked eBay: Loose Fluffs range from $10.00 to $70.00, while NRFB Fluffs go for $200.00, so it looks like Fluff's stock has risen in the last decade or so."

Wendy Vardaman, Madison, WI, is the author of *Obstructed View* (Fireweed Press) and the co-editor/webmaster of *Verse Wisconsin*. She has a PhD in English from University of Pennsylvania and a BS in Engineering from Cornell University. Her poems, reviews, and interviews have appeared in a variety of anthologies and journals, including *Poetry Daily; Breathe: 101 Contemporary Odes; Riffing on Strings: Creative Writing Inspired by String Theory; Poet Lore; Qarrtsiluni; Rain Taxi Review; RATTLE;* and *Portland Review*. She works for the children's theater, The Young Shakespeare Players.

A National Endowment for the Arts Fellow, **Martha Vertreace-Doody** is Distinguished Professor of English and Poet-in-Residence at Kennedy-King College. She received her MFA at Vermont College. Her books include *Second House from* the *Corner; Under a Cat's-Eye Moon; Oracle Bones; Cinnabar; Smokeless Flame; Kelly in the Mirror; Maafa: When Night Becomes a Lion; Dragon Lady: Tsukimi;* and *Glacier Fire. Light Caught Bending* and *Second Mourning*, published by Diehard Publishers, Edinburgh, won Scottish Arts Council Grants. Named the *Glendora Review* Poet, Lagos, Nigeria, she was twice a Fellow at the Hawthornden International Writers' Retreat, Scotland, and Poetry Fellow at the Writers Center, Dublin, Ireland. She and her father collected shells for many years, always listening for the song of sea within them.

Helen Pruitt Wallace's book, *Shimming the Glass House* (Ashland Poetry Press, 2008), won the Richard Snyder Prize and a Florida Book Award. Wallace received her PhD in English/Creative Writing from Florida State University and is Assistant Professor of Creative Writing at Eckerd College in St. Petersburg, FL. Along with occasional Indian artifacts, like most writers, she collects odd images scribbled on the backs of torn envelopes and cocktail napkins, some of which (if she's lucky) find their ways into poems.

Andrea L. Watson's poetry has appeared in *RUNES, Cream City Review, Nimrod, Plath Profiles, International Poetry Review, The Dublin Quarterly* and *Memoir (and)*, and is forthcoming in *RHINO* and *Spillway*. Her show, *Braided Lives: A Collaboration Between Artists and Poets*, founded with artist Seamus Berkeley, was inaugurated by the Taos Institute of Arts and has traveled to San Francisco, Denver, and Berkeley. She has designed and curated sixteen *ekphrasis* events across the United States, including *Interwoven Illuminations; Reflections on RANE; Threaded Lives: Poems from the Fiber World; Frida.Fractured.;* and, most recently, with artist David Hinske, *Fragments: Poets and Artists of the South and Southwest*. With co-author, Madelyn Garner, her chapter on *ekphrasis* appears in the new anthology, *Wingbeats: Exercises & Practice in Poetry* (Dos Gatos Press, 2011). She was one of the founding publishers, and editor, of *HeartLodge: Honoring the House of the Poet.*

"I collect photographs, mirrors, poems, jewelry, costumes, candles—even altars—dedicated to Frida Kahlo. Diego only figures in one of them."

Will Wells is a college English professor in Ohio. His first book, *Conversing with the Light*, won the Anhinga Award, and his second book, *Unsettled Accounts* (Ohio University Press), won the 2009 Hollis Summers Prize. He has published his poems and translations widely in the United States and the United Kingdom. Wells does *not* collect buttons, though his grandmother did. He *does* collect a range of items, including books, Renaissance furniture and carvings, Italian majolica, fossils, North American artifacts, lithographs, and postcards. As a child, Wells aspired to create his own museum, and as his collecting habits indicate, he is working towards that dream though limited by space. Believing poetry is an act of preservation, he collects other items which also relate to preservation.

Scott Wiggerman is the author of two books of poetry, *Presence* (Pecan Grove Press, 2011) and *Vegetables and Other Relationships*. Recent publications include *Switched-on Gutenberg, BorderSenses, 14 x 14, Poemeleon, Broad River Review, Boxcar Poetry Review, Assaracus*, and *Southwestern American Literature*. A frequent workshop instructor, he also is an editor for Dos Gatos Press, publisher of the annual *Texas Poetry Calendar*, now in its fourteenth year, and publisher of the new book, *Wingbeats: Exercises and Practice in Poetry*, co-edited with David Meischen.

"The italicized words in 'The Words I Carry' all come from my Personal Universe Deck. (Google the term for directions on creating your own! Highly recommended!)"

John Willson is a recipient of a Pushcart Prize and awards from the Academy of American Poets, the Pacific Northwest Writers Conference, the Artist Trust of Washington, and The King County Arts Commission. His chapbook, *The Son We Had*, was published by Blue Begonia Press. Willson's poems have appeared in such journals as *Bellevue Literary Review, California Quarterly, Cold Mountain Review, Journal of the American Medical Association, Kyoto Journal, Northwest Review, Notre Dame Review, Poet Lore*, and *Sycamore Review*, and in anthologies, including *Under Our Skin: Literature of Breast Cancer* and *Spreading the Word: Editors on Poetry*. A two-time finalist in the National Poetry Series, he lives on Bainbridge Island, WA where he is employed as a poetry workshop instructor and as a bookseller at an independent bookstore. Willson collects rubber stamps and aloha shirts.

Gary Young is a poet and artist whose books include *Hands; The Dream of a Moral Life*, which won the James D. Phelan Award; *Days; Braver Deeds*, winner of the Peregrine Smith Poetry Prize; and *No Other Life*, which won the William Carlos Williams Award. His most recent books are *Pleasure* and *Bear Flag Republic: Prose Poems and Poetics from California*. Young's *New and Selected Poems* is forthcoming from White Pine Press. He has received a Pushcart Prize, a fellowship from the National Endowment for the Humanities, two fellowships from the National Endowment for the Arts, and the Shelley Memorial Award from the Poetry Society of America. Young edits the Greenhouse Review Press, and his print work is represented in many collections, including the Museum of Modern Art and the Getty Center for the Arts. He teaches at the University of California Santa Cruz and lives with his wife and sons in the mountains north of Santa Cruz.

Paula Anne Yup was first published freshman year in a magazine entitled *CQ* after encouragement from its editor, Dr. Kenneth Atchity, who taught at Occidental College, her alma mater. Over eight hundred submissions later, she has had poems published in *The Third Woman: Minority Women Writers of the United States; Passages North Anthology; What Book!?;* Outrider Press anthologies; and other places. Yup was born in Phoenix, AZ and attended college in Los Angeles, CA and Montpelier, VT.

"Here in the Republic of the Marshall Islands, I sat in on a class of P. K. Harmon's, and 'Have Some Tea' is the result of a shattered narrative assignment. I think the poem has a small selection of some people who have taken my attention and left me disconcerted and off-kilter in my journey through life."

Kristin Camitta Zimet is the editor of *The Sow's Ear Poetry Review* and the author of a poetry collection, *Take in My Arms the Dark.* Her poems are in numerous anthologies and magazines, among them *Lullwater Review, Crab Orchard Review, Salt Hill,* and *Red Cedar.* She sets poems to music and has performed them from Texas to Connecticut. Zimet also works as a nature guide in the Shenandoah Valley of Virginia. Her husband says she collects "everything", but mostly this means things without price: companionable poems, peculiar words, second-hand fantasy books, mountain trails, seeds and seedpods of native plants, rocks, bird songs, deep friends, and old big dogs in need of rescue. Also grandchildren, musical instruments, sunrises, and clouds.

Acknowledgments

M. Lee Alexander, "Tintin Saves the World," from *Observatory,* (Finishing Line Press). Copyright © 2007 by M. Lee Alexander. Reprinted by permission of the author.

Antler, "Dachau Stone" originally appeared in *New York Quarterly.* It was published in *Antler: The Selected Poems,* (Soft Shell Press). Copyright © 2000 by Antler. Reprinted by permission of the author.

Gustavo Adolfo Aybar, "The Only Thing I Have," printed by permission of the author.

Jackie Bartley, "On a Panel from the Art Cupboard of Philipp Hainhofer Presented to Gustavus Adolphus in 1612," printed by permission of the author.

Jeanne Marie Beaumont, "Photographing the Dolls," from *Placebo Effects,* by Jeanne Marie Beaumont. Copyright © 1997 by Jeanne Marie Beaumont. Used by permission of W. W. Norton & Company, Inc.

Robin Becker, "The Miniaturists," from *Domain of Perfect Affection*, by Robin Becker, © 2006. Reprinted by permission of the University of Pittsburgh Press.

Candace Black, "Blue and White," printed by permission of the author.

Sean Brendan-Brown, "Holiday List," printed by permission of the author.

Christopher Buckley, "Cloud Collecting," printed by permission of the author.

William K. Buckley, "Composure," printed by permission of the author.

Kathryn Stripling Byer, "Lauds," printed by permission of the author.

Marcus Cafagña, "Beer Can Wranglers," originally titled "Wayne," from *Poetry Center 1989 Anthology* (1989). Reprinted by permission of the author.

Kathleen Cain, "Finding Daisies," printed by permission of the author.

Kevin Carollo, "I'm starting a plastic menagerie," printed by permission of the author.

Alex Cigale, "In the still forest heard from far away," was published in *Qarrtsiluni* (2010). Reprinted by permission of the author.

Nicole Cooley, "At the Corning Museum of Glass," printed by permission of the author.

Peter R. Cooley, "Afterwards," from *Divine Margins*, (Carnegie Mellon University Press). Copyright © 2009 by Peter Cooley. Reprinted by permission of Carnegie Mellon University Press.

Barbara Daniels, "Collecting," printed by permission of the author.

Joshua Doležal, "Two Memories," printed by permission of the author.

Wendy Drexler, "Adam," a section from "Voices from the Garden," *Freshwater* (2009). Reprinted by permission of the author.

Denise Duhamel, "$500,000," from *Ka-Ching!*, by Denise Duhamel, © 2009. Reprinted by permission of the University of Pittsburgh Press.

Susan J. Erickson, "Waking on All Souls' Day," printed by permission of the author.

John Fitzpatrick, "Creation," printed by permission of the author.

Sharon Foley, "The Urn," printed by permission of the author.

CB Follett, "Word Gathering," originally appeared in *In Posse Review* (Winter 2008). Reprinted by permission of the author.

Madelyn Garner, "How He Came To Treasure Her," was published in *Dogwood* (Spring 2009). Reprinted by permission of the author.

Veronica Golos, "The Collector," printed by permission of the author.

Kimiko Hahn, "Swinburne Island," from *Toxic Flora*, by Kimiko Hahn. Copyright © 2010 by Kimiko Hahn. Used by permission of W. W. Norton & Company, Inc.

Quinton Hallett, "Worry People," printed by permission of the author.

Michael Hanner, "Philately," was published in *Dona Nobis Pacem* (2006). Reprinted by permission of the author.

James Harms, "Making Up for Lost Time," printed by permission of the author.

Mark D. Hart, "Sap Guys," printed by permission of the author.

Marie Henry, "Onions," from *bite to eat place: an anthology of contemporary food poetry and poetic prose* (Redwood Coast Press). Copyright © 1995. Reprinted by permission of the author.

Mary Crockett Hill, "A Theory of Everything," originally appeared in *RHINO* (2007). It was published in *A Theory of Everything*, (Autumn House Press). Copyright © 2009 by Mary Crockett Hill. Reprinted by permission of Autumn House Press.

Jane Hirshfield, "On the Beach," from *The Lives of the Heart* by Jane Hirshfield. Copyright © 1997 by Jane Hirshfield. Reprinted by permission of HarperCollins Publishers.

Paul Hostovsky, "Naughton's Quarters," originally appeared in *Frigg* (Winter 2008). It was published in *A Little in Love a Lot* (Main Street Rag). Copyright © 2011 by Paul Hostovsky. Reprinted by permission of the author.

Christina Hutchins, "ONE-A-DAY Plus Iron," originally appeared in *Cream City Review*. It was published in *Collecting Light* (Acacia Books). Copyright © 1999 by Christina Hutchins. Reprinted by permission of the author.

Joseph Hutchison, "At the Arts Fundraiser," from *House of Mirrors* (James Andrews & Co, Inc.). Copyright © 1992 by Joseph Hutchison. Reprinted by permission of the author.

Jayne Fenton Keane, "Grandma's Gorgeous Fossilized Bones," from *Not A Muse* (Haven Books). Copyright © 2009 by Jayne Fenton Keane. Reprinted by permission of the author.

Susan Kenyon, "Offal," printed by permission of the author.

Christian Knoeller, "Hoosier Histories," printed by permission of the author.

William Kupinse, "Room," from *Fallow*, (Exquisite Disarray). Copyright © 2009 by William Kupinse. Reprinted by permission of the author.

J. Keiko Lane, "Excavations," printed by permission of the author.

Wayne Lee, "White Glass," printed by permission of the author.

Rebecca Lehmann, "The Riddle Game," printed by permission of the author.

Lyn Lifshin, "One More Woman In Love With Old Maps," printed by permission of the author.

Ellaraine Lockie, "Wellspring," printed by permission of the author.

Cheryl Loetscher, "What Can Be Done With Words," printed by permission of the author.

Laura LeHew, "The Chest," printed by permission of the author.

Rachel Loden, "A Lending Library," from *Dick of the Dead*, (Ahsahta Press). Copyright © 2009 by Rachel Loden. Reprinted by permission of Ahsahta Press.

Christina Lovin, "Paper Doll Ghazal," printed by permission of the author.

Alexander Lumans, "At Night, the Valentine Armadillo Hides Valentine Cards," printed by permission of the author.

Marie-Elizabeth Mali, "Refraction," printed by permission of the author.

Marjorie Manwaring, "Reappearing," originally appeared in *Sentence: a journal of prose poetics* (2005). It was published in *Magic Word* (Pudding House Publications). Copyright © 2007 by Marjorie Manwaring. Reprinted by permission of the author.

Karla Linn Merrifield, "One Hard Lesson," was published in *Boatman's Quarterly Review* (Summer 2003). Reprinted by permission of the author.

John O'Dell, "Of Petrified Wood, Arrowheads, and Doorways," printed by permission of the author.

Jessy Randall, "Rare Blue Mad Boy," printed by permission of the author.

Carlos Reyes, "Estate," from *The Book of Shadows: New and Selected Poems,* by Carlos Reyes, © 2009, first published by Lost Horse Press. Reprinted by permission of Lost Horse Press (www.losthorsepress.org).

Jonathan Rice, "Aqua Accelerando," was published in *Pebble Lake Review 5* (Fall/Winter 2007). Reprinted by permission of the author.

Pattiann Rogers, "The Composer, The Bone Yard," by Pattiann Rogers, from *Song of the World Becoming: New and Collected Poems 1981-2001.* (Minneapolis: Milkweed Editions, 2001). Copyright © 2001 by Pattiann Rogers. Reprinted with permission from Milkweed Editions (www.milkweed.org).

Marjorie Saiser, "Rooms," from *Rooms* (Pudding House Publications). Copyright © 2010 by Marjorie Saiser. Reprinted by permission of the author.

Penelope Scambly Schott, "Morpho," originally appeared in *Natural Bridge* (2010). It was published in *Crow Mercies* (CALYX Books). Copyright © 2010 by Penelope Scambly Schott. Reprinted by permission of the author.

Peter Schwartz, "portraiture," was published in *Diagram* (2010).

Nancy Scott, "On Bidding Up a Rug on eBay," from *Detours & Divisions* (Main Street Rag). Copyright © 2011 by Nancy Scott. Reprinted by permission of the author.

Paula Sergi, "Gardener," printed by permission of the author.

Julia Meylor Simpson, "The Collection," printed by permission of the author.

Nancy Simpson, "The Collection," was published in *Night Student* (State Street Press). Copyright © 1985 by Nancy Simpson. Later, in *Living Above the Frost Line: New and Selected Poems* (Carolina Wren Press, Laurel Series). Copyright © 2010 by Nancy Simpson. Reprinted by permission of the author.

John Oliver Simon, "Isla Negra," appeared in *Poetry Flash* (February 1993). Reprinted by permission of the author.

Su Smallen, "A Quieter Art," was published in *Weight of Light* (Laurel Poetry Collective). Copyright © 2004 by Su Smallen. Reprinted by permission of the author.

Mark Smith-Soto, "From the Back of the Closet," printed by permission of the author.

David Spiering, "A String of Buttons as Prayer Beads," printed by permission of the author.

Joseph Stanton, "Shibata Zshin's *Monkey Posing as a Collector,*" appeared online in *The Journal of Mythic Arts* (Winter 2007). Reprinted by permission of the author.

Carol Steinhagen, "Botanica," printed by permission of the author.

Fiona Sze-Lorrain, "Shoebox Filled with Mao Buttons," was published in *Ellipsis* (Spring 2009). Reprinted by permission of the author.

Katrin Talbot, "My Bloody Acquaintances," printed by permission of the author.

Susan Terris, "The Dust-Collector Considers Fly-Fishing For Sharks," appeared in *Pudding Magazine* (2004). Reprinted by permission of the author.

Diane Thiel, "Textiles" from *Echolocations* (Story Line Press). Copyright © 2000 by Diane Thiel. Reprinted by permission of the author.

David Trinidad, "Fluff," from *Plasticville* (Turtle Point Press). Copyright © 2000 by David Trinidad. Reprinted by permission of Turtle Point Press.

Wendy Vardaman, "Mother Contemplates the Creator's Refrigerator," appeared in *The Mom Egg* (2011). Reprinted by permission of the author.

Martha Vertreace-Doody, "Naming Shells," printed by permission of the author.

Helen Pruitt Wallace, "Trappings," originally appeared in *Penumbra* (1997). It was published in *Shimming the Glass House* (Ashland Poetry Press). Copyright © 2008 by Helen Pruitt Wallace. Reprinted by permission of the author.

Andrea L. Watson, "the altar of one dark eyebrow," originally appeared in *RUNES, A Review of Poetry*, "Hearth" (Winter 2006). Reprinted by permission of the author.

Will Wells, "Allegiances in Cora's Room," printed by permission of the author.

Scott Wiggerman, "The Words I Carry," printed by permission of the author.

John Willson, "Memory Jug," printed by permission of the author.

Gary Young, "The shallow stream murmurs," from *Pleasure*. Copyright © 2006 by Gary Young. Reprinted by permission of the author and Heyday Books.

Paula Anne Yup, "Have Some Tea," appeared online in 5th *Gear* (2008). Reprinted by permission of the author.

Kristin Camitta Zimet, "Collecting," was published in *Cold Mountain Review* (Spring 1997). Reprinted by permission of the author.